BODY PARTS

BODY PARTS

A British Serial Killer in Singapore

TAN OOI BOON

TIMES BOOKS INTERNATIONAL
Singapore • Kuala Lumpur

Photographs courtesy of the Singapore Police Force except on Pages 83 (top) and 85 (top), by the author.

Published by Times Books International,
an imprint of Times Editions Pte Ltd.
Times Centre
1 New Industrial Road
Singapore 536196

Times Subang
Lot 46, Subang Hi-Tech Industrial Park
Batu Tiga, 40000 Shah Alam
Selangor Darul Ehsan, Malaysia

Printed in Singapore

ISBN 981 204 693 3

To the men and women of the Singapore Police Force who keep criminals like John Martin off our streets.

CONTENTS

Foreword *8*

1. The Discovery *11*
2. Picking Up The Trail *20*
3. The Pieces Come Together *27*
4. Fatal Journey *37*
5. The Killer in Phuket, Thailand *61*
6. Arrest in Singapore *97*
7. Dead Men Tell Tales *108*
8. Preparation For Trial *117*
9. My British Friend and I *129*
10. Going for the Killer *145*
11. To Dissect a Killer *158*
12. Death of a Killer *182*
13. Profile of a Serial Killer *188*

About the Author *199*

Acknowledgements *200*

FOREWORD

The "body parts" murder was one of the most shocking crimes ever committed in Singapore. Perhaps it was because the perpetrator was a serial killer who cold-bloodedly dismembered the body of his victim. He was a master criminal who knew what he wanted and how to get it.

John Martin roamed the streets freely for several days after killing his victims in hotel rooms. He mingled with many people. One even visited him in his room for more than an hour. Yet, no one suspected anything—partly because Martin was a soft-spoken and charming man by nature and partly because he was a convincing actor.

He was caught because of two mistakes. He picked the wrong victim in Singapore, one who was missed by his family in South Africa. He also underestimated the mettle of the Singapore Police Force. The key investigators—Assistant Superintendent Gerald Lim, Staff Sergeant Zainal Abidin and Inspector Zainudin Lee—were so meticulous that their research spanned six countries: Singapore, Thailand, Indonesia, Britain, Canada and

South Africa. Their work earned praise from the Singapore High Court; testimony that thorough police investigation is crucial in solving complex crimes.

In writing *Body Parts*, I have tried to be as accurate as possible. However, there were certain events that only the killer and his victims would ever know. For these, I have reconstructed fair accounts based on evidence, research and police deduction.

Even hardened crime reporters will confess that it is never easy to write about the suffering of defenceless victims and their families. It is more so when the suffering is the result of a gruesome and heinous crime.

In the course of covering Martin's case, I had the opportunity to meet a victim's widow in court. I share her grief and hope that no one will ever have to go through her nightmare.

1

THE DISCOVERY

Monday, March 13, 1995

Boatman Lee knew the sea off Clifford Pier; it had been his work place for the past 20 years. His job was to take people where they wanted to go for a fee. That morning, what mattered most to him was to reach home quickly to get some rest. After all, he had been ferrying construction workers to a nearby island since the previous night. It was after 10 am and he was about 100 m from the jetty when a floating object bumped against his boat. Wondering what it could be, he stuck his neck out for a better look and saw something that would give him recurring nightmares: a black plastic garbage bag tied with blue underwear, with a human leg protruding out of it.

Pier Master Wong Look Kai had been at his post for slightly more than three hours when the boatman rushed into his office and told him about the grisly find. Wong alerted the Singapore Police Coast Guard immediately, then made his way to the jetty, located at the brink of Singapore's main commercial district, to await police arrival.

Police Coast Guard Corporal Siah Cheong Seng and his crew on patrol boat *PX 15* had been patrolling the coast since early that morning. As law enforcers of the sea, it is routine for them to be called upon to intercept suspicious looking craft in Singapore waters. Occasionally, the intruders are cigarettes smugglers; on other days, they are human traders trying to smuggle illegal immigrants from neighbouring countries into Singapore.

But these are not the only duties of the Coast Guard. Sometimes, the officers investigate crimes off the Singapore mainland. There are also occasions when they are deployed to rescue the victims of accidents at sea—with their speed boats, they are able to reach the scene quickly. The flip side of rescue work, however, is the grim task of recovering corpses. Calamities cannot always be avoided, but sometimes men die at their own hands because they are frustrated with living.

Corpses at sea are not a pretty sight. Decomposition of the human body generates gases that cause it to float. The buoyancy is so strong that criminals who try to hide bodies in the sea by weighing them down with metal objects have found themselves exposed by this force of nature. To the Police Coast Guard, recovering corpses at sea or from a river is just another aspect of their work. The officers have even devised a special net to lift bodies out of the water. Limbs have fallen apart in the past when the bodies were taken on board the patrol craft. With the net, the problem does not arise.

So when the message about the legs was radioed to Cpl Siah and two other crew members on the morning of

March 13, they did not realise that the case would be different and the *PX 15* headed immediately for Clifford Pier. When Cpl Siah and his colleagues reached the scene at about 11 am, Pier Master Wong pointed the bag out to them. It was about 50 m away, near a yellow buoy. As *PX 15* sailed near the bag, waves tossed it up and down. Cpl Siah used a hook to push the bag to the rear of the boat and lift it up. He saw a foot sticking out, although the bag was tied tightly in the centre with a piece of blue underwear. He radioed his operations room about the discovery, after which *PX 15* cruised in the vicinity to look for similar bags. The crew did not find any.

Half an hour later, Sergeant Peter Lim arrived and boarded the patrol boat to inspect the bag, which had been untied by the crew. When he opened it, a foul smell caused him to flinch. There were two decomposed human legs inside, both severed at the knee. There was something sinister about this find.

Eight days earlier, the Police Coast Guard had recovered a cut-off human leg in the vicinity. That limb belonged to a 21-year-old Indonesian worker who was working on a sand barge when his right leg was caught between some cables. The cables sliced the leg off and it dropped into the sea.

But the circumstances surrounding these two legs were different. Someone had wrapped them up carefully before they were thrown away. They would have rested at the bottom of the sea but for gases generated by decomposition, which caused the legs to float to the surface. Rotting of the flesh was fairly advanced, with discoloration and peeling of the skin. The legs were later removed to the Singapore General Hospital mortuary.

The next day, senior pathologist Professor Chao Tzee Cheng performed an autopsy on the legs. He found that both had been cut at the knee joints. They measured 44 cm in length and weighed about 3.5 kg each. The skin was fair with fine brown hair, the toenails short and manicured. The professor's assessment was that the pair of legs belonged to a well-groomed, reasonably well-built, middle-aged male Caucasian. But what struck him was that the upper parts of the legs had clean-cut edges. They had been disarticulated: cut cleanly and twisted out of the bone sockets at the knee joint without damaging the bony ends of the legs.

From his years of experience, including autopsies performed in four other cases in which the victims' bodies had also been chopped up, he concluded that such cuts could only have been executed by an expert. The other cases had been the work of inexperienced killers who used heavy choppers to hack through the bones. The "expert" in the latest case, Professor Chao said, was possibly a doctor, surgeon, veterinarian or butcher. He told police later, "We could be dealing with a serial killer."

In view of the professor's findings, the police classified the case as murder, even though the victim's identity and the whereabouts of the rest of his body were unknown. A statement was issued to the press and those with information were asked to contact the Criminal Investigation Department's Special Investigation Section, the specialist murder-solving squad of the Singapore Police Force.

It was unusual for a case to be classified as murder when only a pair of legs had been found. What about the rest of the body? To the police, however, it is not vital that a corpse be found before they launch an investigation. Criminals have been sent to the gallows even when their victims' bodies were never recovered. But was the owner still alive when his legs were sawed off? If that were so, the case could not be classified as murder.

What turned the fact around was that the legs were indeed cut off after the man had died. The wounds were certified by the professor to be post mortem wounds as there was no reaction, such as bleeding at the tissue, when the legs were cut off. This meant that the man had died before the wounds were inflicted. To the police, it was reason to suspect foul play. It was unlikely that the limbs had come from a hospital or even a funeral parlour.

But although the police had set their course correctly, there was still the task of tracking down the killer. He could be psychotic and extremely dangerous. What if he decided to strike again? The police had to act fast. There was also the nagging question of who the dead man was. The fact that he was Caucasian added another dimension to the mystery as the Singapore population was primarily Asian. Was he a resident? If not, what was he doing in Singapore? Most importantly, why was he killed? These questions were not left unanswered for long. The lead for the police came in the form of a faxed letter dated March 13.

Missing South African Male

This is a serious request for help as the person concerned is very reliable and when away, makes daily contact with family members. It is clear that some event or circumstances are preventing this contact. He arrived in Singapore on South African Airways flight no. SA 282 on Wednesday, March 8, 1995, at 0700 hours. Last contact was in South Africa on boarding the flight. He had arrived in Singapore as purchases had been made on his credit card. He was expected back in South Africa at 0625 hours on March 11, 1995. Please ensure that all police stations and hospitals are notified of the following details:

MISSING PERSON

Surname:	Lowe
First Names:	Gerard George
Age:	33
Hair colour:	Brown (slightly grey)
Approx. height:	1.7 metres (5 feet 7 inches)
Build:	Well built
Race:	White European Male

At the bottom of the letter was an appeal for anyone who knew the man to call his sister, Terry Ingrid Gillett, or parents in South Africa. The telephone numbers of a friend in Singapore and the South African Embassy were included.

I became involved in this case at about the same time, when a copy of the letter was faxed to my newsroom. As a crime reporter with *The Straits Times*, covering murder stories was not new to me. From cases I had encountered, I found that two common reasons could drive a person to kill—money and women.

Some years ago, a robber strangled his neighbour's 10-year-old daughter for only a few thousand dollars. The girl was killed because she was at home and could identify him. In another case, a man stabbed his wife's lover to death after stalking him for a few days. In both cases, the killers met their fate at the end of the rope—one by the process of law and the other by his own hand.

But what came to be dubbed by the press as "the body parts murder" was unlike the other cases I had covered. At that time, the police did not disclose to the media that the killer was an expert with the knife, yet his modus operandi suggested it was a deliberate and well-planned killing.

When I first read the letter from South Africa, I was certain that the missing person was the unidentified murder victim. I came to this conclusion because of the forensic pathologist's description of the legs—that they belonged to a middle-aged Caucasian man—and the fact that the murder case and missing person report were being investigated by the same detective: 37-year-old Staff Sergeant Zainal Abidin Ismail. An officer with close to 20 years' experience, he reminded one of the rugged cops portrayed in movies—streetwise and versatile.

I approached the Singapore Police Force media spokesman, Assistant Superintendent Lim Chin Tiak, of the Public Affairs Department. He was my senior at the

National University of Singapore's Faculty of Law. One of his duties was to provide the media with information on criminal cases in Singapore so that reporters could write accurate reports.

I said to ASP Lim, "I know the cut-up legs belonged to the South African. And I know the police think so too as the investigations are being handled by the same officer. Can I have police confirmation for my story?"

He laughed because I had guessed correctly and was eager to be the first reporter to break the news. He did not reply immediately, but promised to check with the Criminal Investigation Department.

A short while later, he called me in my office and spoke cautiously, "I hope you can delay your report for a few days. The police are in the midst of investigations and do not want to give you an answer at this stage."

I sensed something unusual was happening as the police were usually very forthcoming in answering press queries.

I replied, "I know you guys think my story will get in the way of investigations. I don't see how this can be so but since I am the only one making the inquiry, I am willing to play along. I still want the story and hope you will give it to me when the time is right."

ASP Lim said, "I can't promise you anything now but will check with the CID again." With that, he put down the telephone.

A few minutes later, the phone rang again with ASP Lim on the line, "Okay. No story now but you will be the first to write it when the time is right."

It was not common practice for the police to strike such a deal with a reporter. I did not press further as I knew they had their reasons. I was to find out later that they did not want any media publicity that might alert the killer. He might have thought that, by dismembering the body, the identities of both the victim and himself would remain a mystery.

The killer had already left Singapore but the police were certain he would return—perhaps to look for another victim. They were waiting for him.

2

PICKING UP THE TRAIL

Tuesday, March 14

When the police received the letter from South Africa, they knew it was an important clue and acted immediately. Armed with the name of the victim and his flight number, Sgt Peter Lim's first stop was at the Singapore Hotel Association, which was asked to check if a Gerard George Lowe had checked into any of the hotels in Singapore. The association contacted its members and established that he had checked into the River View Hotel in Havelock Road on March 8, five days before the legs were discovered. The hotel is located beside the Singapore River, which flows into the sea at Clifford Pier not far away.

By this time, a senior CID investigator, Assistant Superintendent Gerald Lim Han Ming, 33, had joined in the investigation. Although ASP Lim had been with the police for only five years, he had acquired a reputation for being a competent and meticulous investigator. It was not unusual for him to work 18-hour days, every day of the week, when he was hot on the trail of a criminal.

At about noon on March 14, after being briefed on the missing South African, ASP Lim and Staff Sgt Zainal Abidin went to the River View Hotel. There, they learned from the front office that Lowe did not check into the hotel alone on March 8. He was with another man, Simon Davis, who held a British passport. Both men shared Room 1511.

While going through the records, the officers saw that Lowe's name was taken off the guest register one day later, on March 9. And Davis, who settled the bills, checked out alone on March 11. After that, Room 1511 was let out to an Indonesian couple who stayed for three nights. They left the hotel before the officers arrived.

Sensing that Davis was a key suspect in the case, ASP Lim gave orders for the name to be put at the top of the police list of wanted persons. Any person who produced a passport with this name at any of Singapore's entry or exit points would be detained. The officers then took the keys and went up to Room 1511.

They detected a musty smell in the room as soon as they entered. The room, and especially the bedcovers, was in disarray as the chambermaids had not cleaned up after the last guests left. The officers made a quick search, checking the beds, carpet, walls, cupboards and drawers. Nothing incriminating was found. There were no bloodstains or other signs to suggest foul play.

The officers proceeded to the bathroom and found nothing amiss at first glance. Closer inspection, however, revealed fine blood splatters on the wall tiles opposite the shower head. The officers held their breath: despite possibly crucial evidence being washed away by three days of bathing by the last guests, there were still telltale signs. Something terrible must have occurred for the stains to remain this long. The officers looked harder and every corner was checked. When they closed the bathroom door behind them, they saw more specks of blood all over the door and on the wall beside it.

Staff Sgt Zainal Abidin then lay on the bathroom floor to get a different view. He looked up and, as expected, saw blood below the toilet bowl. It was a fairly big splatter too. No one had thought of cleaning this inconspicuous spot—not the chambermaids, and not even the killer.

As the bloodstains supported the suggestion of foul play, the CID's Scene of Crime Unit officers were called in to take photographs and a sketch plan of the room was drawn. Officers took swabs of the bloodstains so that DNA tests could be conducted later to identify the victim. While Staff Sgt Zainal Abidin directed the investigations in the hotel room, ASP Lim returned to the reception counter to ask for all documents related to Room 1511, such as the invoice, and telephone and restaurant bills. The papers might reveal the movements or certain acts of the tenants during their stay. He also gave orders to seal off Room 1511 so that no one except the police could enter. The room was not to be disturbed because it might contain other important clues to a suspected murder.

Later that evening, with a heavy heart, ASP Lim telephoned Lowe's sister, Terry Gillett, in South Africa. He broke the news to her, saying that the Singapore police had reason to suspect her brother had been murdered, and his body dismembered and thrown into the sea. He also told her that police had found a pair of legs which possibly belonged to him. As the victim's identity could not be confirmed, he asked her to provide blood samples from relatives for DNA profiling to be done.

It was a big blow to Terry as she had not given up hope that her brother was alive. His wife, Vanessa, had also been hopeful. Checks with his bank showed that his credit card had been used in Singapore. To both women, this was an indication that he was still alive because he appeared to be using his credit card. Or was he? After the initial shock, Terry volunteered to send her own blood sample for the DNA tests. She said it would arrive in Singapore the next day. She also furnished ASP Lim with records of Lowe's credit card transactions in Singapore.

Wednesday, March 15

ASP Gerald Lim started his day early as he was going to meet someone at Changi International Airport at about 7.30 am. That person was Marita Badenhorst from South Africa. She was coming to Singapore for a holiday, but had with her a very important package. Before she left South Africa, Terry Gillett had given her three test tubes containing her own blood sample, and two photographs of the missing man, Gerard George Lowe.

Back at his office, ASP Lim handed the test tubes to Staff Sgt Zainal Abidin. These would be sent to the Department of Scientific Services where DNA tests would be conducted to determine if the decomposed legs belonged to the South African man.

DNA is an organic material found in cells throughout the human body. It is the same regardless of which part of the body it is taken from. For example, the DNA of an individual's blood, tissues, hair roots, bone marrow and body fluid, such as semen, is the same. Apart from this characteristic, DNA carries genetic codes inherited from one's parents. This means that DNA samples from two close relatives, such as a brother and sister, should contain some similarities.

This was what the Singapore police had hoped to achieve by obtaining the blood sample from Terry Gillett—to determine if the dead man was indeed her brother. Also, except for identical twins, each person's DNA is unique, making it an invaluable tool for identifying an unknown murder victim. In this case, police could match the DNA of Terry's blood, that of blood found in the bathroom of the River View Hotel room and DNA from the severed legs to determine whether they contained any similarities. If the tests were all positive, then Lowe had indeed been killed and the crime possibly took place in the hotel room.

Back in their office, the detectives went through the River View Hotel invoice for Room 1511, seized the previous day. They found records of telephone calls made from the room on March 9 and 10. Most were local calls but one was made to a number in Britain. It was traced to the Thomas Cook Traveller's Cheques office in Peterborough, Britain. Further checks revealed that a call was also made to the Thomas Cook office in Anson Road, Singapore.

At about noon, ASP Lim and Staff Sgt Zainal Abidin arrived at the Thomas Cook office. They introduced themselves to the employees, saying that they were investigating a crime, and asked for their assistance. During questioning, delivery clerk Tangis Sulaiman said he had found a carrier bag on the sofa in the reception area on March 13. He gave the green-purple-black bag to ASP Lim, who opened it and was overwhelmed by a foul smell. Inside the bag was a document bag, a bottle of Lynx deodorant and a sales receipt for the deodorant, bought from the Smart Supermarket at Marina Square, a shopping mall facing the sea at Marina Bay. Someone had sprayed the deodorant into the bag, as if trying to mask the odour. The document bag was blue and imprinted with the words "Institute of Breweries of South Africa".

ASP Lim showed the colour photographs of Lowe to the employees. None recalled having met the man but when he asked about Simon Davis, a flood of information came out. The man had visited the office a few times to conduct various transactions. These included reporting missing traveller's cheques, transmitting money to a bank account in the United States and buying a return air ticket to Bangkok. So the suspect might return to Singapore. There was a good chance of catching him if he did not know the police were waiting for him.

From Thomas Cook, the officers obtained a photocopy of Davis's British passport. On it was a stamp indicating that it was issued by the British High Commission in Singapore on March 10, only five days ago. Now, here was a chance to obtain a photograph of Davis from the

British High Commission. The police were going to know what he looked like.

After leaving Thomas Cook, the officers decided to return to the River View Hotel. There might be some clues they had overlooked in Room 1511. This time, they combed the carpet for bloodstains. The officers applied the Kestle Meyer test on the carpet. Police around the world use this test to look for traces of blood at the scene of a crime. It involves the use of sensitive solutions that react chemically when blood is present. When applied on any surface, the colourless solution turns pinkish red if traces of blood are detected, even if the blood had dried for weeks.

But despite checking the carpet of Room 1511 carefully, the officers did not find any blood. They went into the bathroom and examined the shower curtain again. During the previous check, they could have been distracted by the other bloodstains. This time, they looked carefully from the top to the bottom of the curtain, and their efforts paid off. At the top of the curtain was a single spot of dried blood.

3

THE PIECES COME TOGETHER

Thursday, March 16

Customs officers Mohammed Yahaya Kadri and Zainal Don were on duty at the Customs Harbour Branch headquarters near Clifford Pier. They had started work from 10 pm the previous night and their shift was to end at 8 am that morning.

At about 7.55 am, CO Zainal Don went to the mooring area to make one last check before handing the watch over to the next shift. While counting the number of launches, he saw a black plastic bag, tied with orange cloth, floating at the stern of one of the boats. Wondering what it was, he used a hook to draw the bag closer and open part of it. What he saw was rotting human flesh; at the same time, a foul smell gagged him, causing him to stagger backwards. He composed himself and ran to his office to call the police. Police officers arrived and opened the bag to find a pair of decomposed human thighs inside.

Meanwhile, at about 8.45 am, Police Coast Guard Warrant Officer Kasinathan, Constable Lim Kian Heng and Reservist Staff Sgt Mohammed Rafi were patrolling near the Southern Islands when they were radioed by their operations room. Their orders were to proceed to Clifford Pier to look for black plastic bags floating in the sea.

Half an hour later, near Clifford Pier, PC Lim spotted two such bags. He used a hook to bring the bags onto the deck of the craft. The smaller bag was opened first and there was nothing inside but rubbish and engine oil. Inside the bigger bag, however, was a human torso. One side of the bag was slightly torn and maggots were crawling out of it. The smell was intolerable.

ASP Gerald Lim arrived soon after. He viewed the grisly finds, then gave orders for the torso and thighs to be taken to the Singapore General Hospital mortuary for an autopsy. He did not have to wait for the report to know that the severed parts were also the remains of the missing South African man.

At the morgue, the torso and thighs were examined by Professor Chao Tzee Cheng. The torso, which came from a male adult, had been disarticulated at both the shoulder and hip joints. The head had been cut off at the upper end of the neck. The torso measured 73 cm long and 40 cm wide, and weighed about 50 kg. The skin was fair and had fine brown hair. The head and limbs appeared to have been cut off with a sharp instrument. As with the legs, dismemberment occurred after the victim had died.

There were some identification features on the torso, such as a small mole on the right shoulder, a small scar on the right chest and an appendectomy scar. The penis had also been circumcised. There were no wounds on the body, although two deep marks ran around the torso as a result of being tied too tightly with string. Some black oil stained the back. When the professor dissected the neck, he found some bleeding caused by impact injuries—blows or strong grips—on the neck, but the injuries were not severe enough to cause death.

When the torso was cut open, the internal organs were in an advanced stage of decomposition. However, everything appeared normal and there were no fractures. The stomach was empty, indicating that the victim had not eaten a few hours before his death.

As for the thighs, the left one measured 42 cm in length while the right was 39 cm. Together, they weighed 23 kg and had been dissected expertly at the joint by a sharp instrument. The skin was fair and had fine brown hair. Like the torso, the thighs were in an advanced stage of decomposition and the skin was peeling. The parts could have been dismembered a week or more before the examination.

Prof. Chao's finding was that all the parts—torso, thighs and legs—were from the same person because they were visually similar and the joints fit. The victim was a male Caucasian adult, reasonably well-built and well-groomed (the toenails were well-manicured), weighing more than 70 kg and about 170 cm in height. Without the head, the professor was unable to determine the cause of death. There were impact injuries on the neck and the back of the body but none of them could have caused death. It was very likely that the fatal wound was inflicted on the head, which was still missing.

On the same day, Staff Sgt Zainal Abidin paid a visit to the British High Commission. He told officials there that the police were investigating a crime that possibly involved a British national by the name of Simon Davis. He said this man had recently applied for a replacement passport and asked to see the application form, which was handed to him.

Staff Sgt Zainal Abidin studied the black and white photograph on the form. Davis looked like a stout man, judging from his rather meaty face. In the photograph, he had curly hair, looked serious and did not smile, his deep-set eyes just staring at the camera lens. Staff Sgt Zainal Abidin used his own camera to take pictures of the passport photograph.

Back at his office, he gave the photographs to ASP Gerald Lim and they sat down to discuss the next stage of their investigations. Earlier, they had looked at the details of credit card transactions in Singapore provided by Terry Gillett. The information showed the amount of purchases and serial numbers, but not the points of transaction. There were also three cash withdrawals, totalling $8,400, made at a DBSBank in Singapore. Staff Sgt Zainal Abidin went to the bank's main office to obtain information on where the transactions had taken place.

The officers then decided to split up to conduct the probe separately. Staff Sgt Zainal Abidin would go back to the River View Hotel to interview the staff for more information, while ASP Lim would visit Raffles City Shopping Centre, where almost all the credit card transactions had taken place.

At about 2.40 pm, ASP Lim arrived at the Raffles City Shopping Centre in Stamford Road, not far from Orchard Road. It is one of the main shopping centres in Singapore and its name is familiar to many tourists, for at the same site stands the world's tallest hotel, the 73-storey Westin Stamford. ASP Lim was, however, not going to the hotel that day. His first stop was the DBSBank. There, he asked for the three credit card transaction slips that reflected cash advances of $8,400 made on the gold Standard Bank MasterCard of Gerard George Lowe.

Meanwhile, at the River View Hotel, Staff Sgt Zainal Abidin was talking to the hotel security guards. One of them, Jamil Snane, had been on duty on the morning of March 11, the day Davis checked out. The officer produced a black and white photograph of Davis, whom Jamil recognised as the Caucasian he had seen in the hotel lobby at about 6 am on March 11. He told the officer he saw the man lugging a big black suitcase out of the hotel.

He said, "I recall telling the bellhop that the man had left the hotel without producing his check-out slip, but the bellhop ignored me so I returned to my duty."

About 15 minutes later, the same man returned to the hotel, this time without the suitcase. Jamil said the man, who was wearing a flowery Hawaiian shirt, wiped his shoes on the carpet and walked past him to the lift lobby. After that, he did not see the man again.

Staff Sgt Zainal Abidin thanked the guard and left. While he was walking out of the hotel, he decided to take a look at the river running behind the building. He walked past the Warehouse Disco next to the hotel and headed towards the river bank. Muddy water was flowing downstream and would eventually reach the sea at Clifford Pier. The officer asked himself what the man could have been doing with the suitcase. What was in it? Could he have been disposing of the chopped-up body parts? The parts that had been found were wrapped in black plastic bags. So what had happened to the suitcase? Staff Sgt Zainal Abidin walked further down the bank, hoping to find what he was looking for. But he did not see the black suitcase.

Friday, March 17

More blood samples arrived from South Africa: from Lowe's mother, Monica, and younger sister, Joanna. These were sent to the Department of Scientific Services for DNA tests.

That afternoon, ASP Gerald Lim returned to the Raffles City Shopping Centre to pick up the paper trail left by Davis when he used Lowe's credit card. His first stop was an electronics shop, Pertama Raffles City. Initial enquiries directed him to Kelvin Lee, one of the salesmen there. When ASP Lim showed him a colour photograph of Lowe, Kelvin could not recall having met such a person. But when the officer showed him Davis's photograph, he said, "That was the man whom I sold a VCR to."

Kelvin also said that the man had wanted to send the video cassette recorder to Britain. This, the officer found out later, was to a Janet Scripps in England. ASP Lim asked for all the credit card transaction slips that Davis had signed at the shop.

The officer's next stop was Sogo Department Store in

the same building. There, he seized transaction slips for the purchase of a pair of Nike shoes and two pairs of socks.

At about 3 pm, he was back at the DBSBank, where he showed photographs of Lowe and Davis to the staff. None could recall seeing either of the men. The bank tellers said they served many people daily—both Asians and Caucasians—and would not be able to remember the faces of all their customers. ASP Lim knew that Davis had been to the bank; his check the previous day had confirmed this. It was a pity no one could remember seeing him—not even the teller who had served him on three occasions. Fortunately, the bank had a closed circuit television camera that recorded all transactions. He asked the bank for a copy of the video recording.

Meanwhile, Staff Sgt Zainal Abidin was called in to investigate what might be a related event. Earlier that day, the Police Coast Guard had received a message that some construction workers had discovered a decomposed human arm wedged among rocks in the sea off Pulau Sudong. The island, about 15 km southwest of Clifford Pier, lies near an area frequently used for live-firing exercises by the military or police. Talk was that this was the missing arm of Lowe and that it had somehow floated to the island.

When police officers arrived at the scene, they saw that the highly decomposed limb was a left arm. It appeared to have been hacked off at the shoulder. The bone of the upper arm was exposed because the flesh had either rotted or been eaten by fish. The lower arm was intact but it was unlikely that fingerprints could be lifted as the fingers were badly decomposed. The officers checked the shore but did not find any other human parts, so they returned to the mainland and handed the limb to the Singapore General Hospital mortuary for an autopsy.

This time, the police were in for a surprise. Forensic tests showed that the arm did not share the same blood type as the torso, thighs and legs of the earlier finds. This meant that the arm did not belong to the South African tourist. If that was so, whose arm was it? Was it the sign of another gruesome killing? While speculation was rife, the police were certain it had nothing to do with the murder in Singapore. They believed that the arm could have floated to the island from a neighbouring country, possibly Indonesia.

Saturday, March 18

Police took photographs of the man, whom they believed to be Davis, off the video recording filmed at the DBSBank. In the footage, a rather tall man, standing at about 1.9 m, is seen signing some papers at the counter before being handed a bundle of notes by the teller. The whole transaction took a while and in that time, the man appeared normal and did not show any sign of nervousness. No one would be able to tell that he was using another man's credit card. A very cool customer indeed.

Sunday, March 19

Five days after investigations began, the two investigators were finally able to take a breather. For Staff Sgt Zainal Abidin, it meant staying at home with his wife and four children. For ASP Gerald Lim, it meant catching up with his girlfriend, whom he had not seen since the probe began. The couple planned a quiet evening—a stroll along the seafront outside the World Trade Centre, followed by dinner. But their plans for the evening were soon disrupted. At about 9.30 pm, Staff Sgt Zainal Abidin received a call at home from the airport police. After getting the necessary information, he hung up and called ASP Lim on the latter's handphone, "We have arrested Simon Davis at the airport."

Monday, March 20

It was a rather slow day for me in the newsroom. At about 6 pm, just as I was about to leave, ASP Lim Chin Tiak called, "I have good news for you. Remember the story about the missing South African that you want to write? You can do it today. The CID will send a statement to you shortly."

I was excited. I did not expect him to get back to me on this topic barely a week after our last conversation. I probed. "So what happened? What will the police say?"

ASP Lim replied, "Wait for the statement, which has all the information you want. The police are confirming the victim's identity. We have also arrested a suspect."

The next day, *The Straits Times* broke the story. The front page report, which showed the photograph of Gerard George Lowe for the first time, read:

Body parts in bags may be those of South African man

The body parts found in plastic bags off Clifford Pier last week are suspected to be those of a South African tourist who arrived in Singapore earlier this month on holiday.

He is said to be Mr Gerard George Lowe, a 33-year-old chemical engineer from Johannesburg, who arrived in Singapore on a shopping trip on March 8. Yesterday, police said a Caucasian man who was found to be holding Mr Lowe's passport and credit cards has been detained for questioning ...

The case involving Singapore's first encounter with a British serial killer had unfolded.

4

FATAL JOURNEY

Gerard George Lowe was the sort of man who would never go to the pub without first informing his wife. He was always considerate and reliable. So it was no surprise that when he was due to go to Singapore alone on March 7, he had a whole list of "instructions" for his wife, Vanessa. After all, it was his first trip to Singapore.

"I will call you the moment I check into a hotel to tell you the contact number of the hotel so that you can call me should there be any problems at home. I plan to find a hotel only on arrival in Singapore. I will be away for three days. If you do not hear from me on March 10, it means that I will have a seat on the plane to return to South Africa and will arrive on March 11. However, if I do call you on March 10, it will be to inform you that I cannot get a seat and will therefore return on March 12."

He was long-winded, but Vanessa was used to it. She knew her husband was a sensible, responsible and well-organised person. They had met in Johannesburg and started dating in October 1989, but were married only on January 9, 1993, after a three-year courtship.

Lowe worked as a chemical engineer in South African Breweries, one of the biggest companies in the country. Vanessa ran a small business making house calls to groom pet dogs. It was something she enjoyed very much. Both she and her husband were dog lovers who owned two Dobermans. Vanessa's Mobile Dog Grooming Service was based at the couple's quiet suburban home in Malanshof, in Randburg, South Africa.

Vanessa and her husband were very close and enjoyed a healthy sexual relationship. He was not the type to swear, not even when he was angry. He was a family man who did not mind washing dishes and doing the laundry to help lighten Vanessa's workload at home. He knew her career was important to her too. They seldom quarrelled and even if they did, were quick to make up.

Although they had no children, they had talked about being parents, and even discussed how they would raise their children. Once, while watching a movie in which one of the characters was a homosexual, Lowe said to his wife that he would disown his son if he turned out to be a homosexual.

He had always wanted to go to Singapore. His friends told him that the country was a shopping paradise. He had heard about Orchard Road, how the whole stretch was lined with big shopping malls, and how cheap the electronic goods were compared with the same items in South Africa. He was not an electronics enthusiast, but had been wanting to replace his 12-year-old Technics hi-fi system that he had owned since his university days. He also wanted to buy a few other items such as a camera, video recorder and perhaps some compact discs.

The thrifty man that he was, he calculated that he would still spend less on these items in Singapore despite having to pay about 900 rands (S$315) for a discounted air ticket and a 20 per cent customs duty on the goods. But he had never made any definite plans to travel to Singapore; he was always too busy with work. In March 1995, the opportunity presented itself.

He was supposed to fly to Zimbabwe to attend a conference from March 6 to 11 but, at the last moment, was told he did not have to go. He saw this as a good time to visit Singapore instead, with Vanessa. The couple often travelled together and their last trip was to Britain, when they had visited Vanessa's relatives and friends. She was supposed to have accompanied Gerard to Zimbabwe too but when the trip was cancelled, she rescheduled all her business appointments to that week. So when Gerard told her about his new plans to visit Singapore and get his shopping done, she did not want to go. It would be too troublesome to change her appointments again. After all, he was only going away for three days and Singapore was reputed to be one of the world's safest cities. What could go wrong? He would be back safely in no time at all, she thought.

Lowe planned to spend about 20,000 rands (S$7,000) on his hi-fi and other electronic goods. When his sisters and friends heard about his Singapore trip, they wanted him to buy things for them as well. One friend wanted a Hewlett Packard calculator. Another asked him to look for a computer circuit board chip, and gave him an old chip as a sample. Vanessa and elder sister Terry wanted binoculars and he would buy various brands of perfume for Terry, younger sister Joanna and another friend. He would also get a telephone answering machine for Joanna to thank her for helping him buy the discounted air ticket.

He planned to fly to Singapore on March 7. The night before he left, he and Vanessa stayed home to pack his luggage. He wanted to bring two bags: one black nylon suitcase to carry his intended purchases and a green-purple-black carrier bag for his own belongings. Inside the suitcase, he packed black plastic trash bags with which to wrap his purchases. As for his clothes, he took mostly casual wear: T-shirts, short-sleeved shirts, bermudas, track pants and several Woolworth's and Edgar's underwear. He knew the weather in Singapore would be warm. In his toiletry pouch, he put in a pair of leather sandals, his digital diary and an asthma inhaler pump—just in case. He was prone to mild asthma attacks.

Lowe asked Vanessa for her black leather waist pouch in which to carry his passport, traveller's cheques and wallet. Inside his black leather wallet, he had some South African notes, a gold Standard Bank MasterCard and various personal cards. He showed Vanessa the US$180 dollar notes he had exchanged with the bank earlier. The bank did not have any Singapore dollars so he decided on US notes that he could change into local currency in Singapore for miscellaneous items such as newspapers or taxi fare.

He had only US$1,120 worth of Thomas Cook traveller's cheques as he intended to charge most of his expenses to his credit card. He borrowed a calculator from Vanessa so that he could do a quick conversion of the exchange rates while shopping.

He also had a clipboard and blue cardboard file in which he noted the prices of various electronic goods in South Africa so that he could compare them with prices in Singapore. Among his notes were a Singapore Tourist Promotion Board brochure containing the names of black-listed shops which overcharged tourists, details of currency conversion rates and the time difference (six hours) between Johannesburg and Singapore. Now he was prepared for his trip.

His flight was scheduled to leave at 3.10 pm on March 7. That morning, he wanted to go to his office for half a day before flying off. He wore an orange collarless T-shirt, beige bermudas, brown belt and deck shoes. Not many people would be in his office as most had flown to Zimbabwe for the conference. His colleague, Rene Heddeger, had promised to drive him to work and to the airport later. Vanessa could not see him off as she had a business appointment.

During breakfast with Vanessa, he was cheerful and excited as he talked about his trip and some of the things he intended to do. He assured her that he would call as soon as he checked into a hotel. Soon, the sound of his colleague's car interrupted their conversation. He kissed his wife goodbye, took his two bags and walked to the front gate. Vanessa waved to him at the door.

Lowe called his wife from the airport but she was not at home. He left a message on the answering machine telling her he had obtained a seat on South African Airlines flight 282 to Singapore. He had initially been put on the standby list as his was a discounted ticket. He said goodbye and told her to take care. Those were his last words to her.

Meanwhile, in Singapore, a tall and well-built Caucasian man arrived at Changi International Airport at about 2 am on March 8. He had come from San Francisco and did not feel tired despite the long flight. He walked out of the arrival hall carrying a black carrier bag. Not many people were around as it was still very early in the day. He frowned; something was on his mind. He walked towards a row of chairs in the main lobby and sat down. He stared hard at people who came out of the arrival hall on early morning flights like his. He twiddled his long fingers and waited.

Not long after, he saw a Caucasian man walking out alone. He looked like a tourist. It was easy to spot tourists. They often appeared lost, looking around for signs and directions. Businessmen or other regular visitors would just walk hurriedly out of the airport and join the taxi queue.

He stood up and approached the man. Wearing his broadest smile, he stuck out his right hand and said, "Hi. I am Simon Davis. How are you?" They shook hands and started talking. He made some gestures and pointed to a few counters at the airport. The man smiled and said something before walking away. He followed and the man stopped to talk again. This time, the man shook his head, smiled and left. He went back to the chairs and sat down.

Lowe was excited. After more than 10 hours' flight, he had finally reached Singapore. After alighting from the plane, he made his way to the Immigration checkpoint. His first impression of Singapore was that everything was so clean. The airport was fully carpeted but there not a single stain or piece of paper on the floor. Soothing classical music was also playing. Clearing the Immigration check was a breeze. He had his passport stamped after waiting for only 15 minutes. And half an hour after he stepped off the plane, he saw his black suitcase and green-purple-black carrier bag on the luggage carousel. No wonder the airport was among the world's best, he thought.

He put his luggage on a trolley and wheeled it out of the arrival hall. After exchanging his US dollars for some Singapore currency, he went to look for a hotel reservation counter. A taxi driver might also be able to recommend a reasonably good hotel, he thought. Before he could decide on his next move, someone tapped him on his shoulder. He turned around and saw a tall, rather handsome and friendly-looking man smiling at him.

The man said, "Hi. I am Simon Davis. How are you?" Lowe greeted him and they shook hands. The man asked whether he was alone and Lowe said yes. The man then suggested travelling and sharing a room together to save costs. They could also keep each other company. He said he was a shopkeeper selling clothes in Mexico and was on his way to Bangkok to buy men's high-fashion clothes. His business was a small one and if he could find a companion with whom to split the hotel charges, he could save some money. Lowe was hesitant but when he heard that the man had been to Singapore several times, he agreed. Perhaps he could recommend the good stores selling electronic products, he thought.

The two then walked to the Singapore Hotel Association's reservation counter. It was about 8 am and reservation clerk Armillah Johar greeted them. The man who had introduced himself as Davis made most of the inquiries. He wanted a room with twin beds, he said, and the hotel should be in Orchard Road. Armillah checked through her records and said that the hotels in Orchard Road were fully booked. He then asked for any hotel near the city.

After making a few telephone calls, Armillah said there was a room in the River View Hotel, which was less than 10 minutes' drive to Orchard Road. The men agreed to take the room. Lowe paid S$10 and the clerk wrote a check-in voucher under his name. After that, the two men joined the taxi queue. About 10 minutes later, they were travelling along the East Coast Parkway on their way to the hotel. During the journey, they talked about themselves. Lowe's companion said he was from Britain.

They arrived at the River View Hotel in Havelock Road at about 9 am. At the check-in counter, senior duty manager Doreen Tan greeted them. Lowe handed her the voucher and said they wanted a room for one night, but might extend the stay for another night. Doreen asked for

S$250 as deposit and the men decided to split the payment. Lowe offered to pay S$130 as the man had paid the taxi fare. Doreen issued a receipt in Lowe's name and gave it to him. But the room was not ready. The hotel was full and many guests had not checked out yet, so she asked the men to return around noon.

Rather than wait idly, Lowe suggested that they make a trip to Orchard Road to check out the shopping centres. His companion agreed. They left their luggage with the hotel and went to look for a taxi.

When the two returned at about noon, Room 1511 was ready. They collected the keys and took a lift to the 15th floor. Lowe felt a sense of relief when he put his bags down in the room. It had been a tiring day and he had not slept well on the plane. Not only that, he had been in and out of several Orchard Road shops just a while ago. "I must be really nuts," he thought, smiling. He had been so eager to shop that he did not even stop for a bite after getting off the plane.

He chose the bed nearest to the window and started to unpack. He was longing for a shower as the weather was warm. As he zipped open his bag, he saw his clipboard resting on top of his clothes. After taking out a T-shirt and underwear, he sat on his bed, facing the window. He started to go through his notes as he wanted to compare the prices of some electronic items that he had seen earlier with the prices of those back home.

So engrossed was he that he failed to notice the evil glint in his companion's eyes. The other man had also started to unpack but some of the items in his black carrier bag were not the things a clothes seller might carry. There were four sharp foldable knives, a heavy hammer weighing 1.5 kg, handcuffs, thumbcuffs and a 40,000-volt electrical stun device. These were the tools of a killer. He glanced at Lowe, still looking at his notes. He took out the stun device and a pair of handcuffs. He then moved ominously closer to the unsuspecting Lowe.

The camera was worth buying. It was about 20 per cent cheaper compared to what he would have to pay in South Africa, Lowe thought. As he went further down his list to check the conversion rates, he saw the information concerning the time difference between South Africa and Singapore. It reminded him that he had to call Vanessa.

As he was about to get up, he suddenly felt a hard object thrust at his neck. It felt as if an iron fist was gripping him even as powerful electrical shocks surged through his body. He fell backwards and hit his back against the table before slumping forward onto the floor. He was barely conscious but could feel someone pulling his arms to his back and securing them with handcuffs. He was too weak to resist but saw that it was the work of his companion. The man dragged him into the bathroom, left him on the floor and closed the door behind them. He then picked up his hammer and raised it.

Thack! The skull cracked. Lowe became motionless and, possibly, lifeless. More importantly, he was silenced. The attacker put down his hammer and looked around. There was blood everywhere. Well, he had expected it; the skin at the scalp had broken upon impact, causing blood to splatter. He checked the man for signs of life. There was none.

He stripped the body, put the orange T-shirt, beige bermudas and light blue underwear aside and carried the body into the bathtub. He took off his own shirt and turned the tap on to wash away the blood on the head. The water was kept running. He took out a foldable knife from the pocket of his trousers and pulled out the sharp blade. He paused, considering which part to go for first. He decided on the head and went straight for the neck, plunging the pointed tip into the cervical bones, then edging the blade into the small crevices between the bones. Forcing the knife downward, he sliced through the flesh in a circular path around the neck. Soon, the head was no longer attached to the neck; it rolled off and dropped with a thud into the bathtub. Blood was oozing slowly from the stump of the neck; there was no heartbeat to pump blood out any faster.

The shoulder joint was next. He was familiar with what he was doing. He pushed the blade deep into the joint until he felt it scraping against the bones. Then he began cutting through the flesh with a circular, sawing motion. He pierced the blade into the socket and turned it around, forcing the bony end of the arm to dislocate. He did the same to the other arm, after which his attention turned to the hip joints. It was like cutting the hindquarter of a cow.

He dug his knife into the pelvic joint and edged the blade around the bony surface. The scraping sound did not bother him. Ten minutes—that was all the time he needed to cut off both legs. But they were still too long and cumbersome so he forced his knife into the kneecaps and cut both legs at the knee joints. The man was no more in less than half an hour.

He splashed water around to wash the blood away. He also used the man's T-shirt to wipe blood off the wall, sink and bathtub. Then he cleaned himself, opened the bathroom door and went into the room. He took the man's suitcase and carrier bag. He opened the suitcase and smiled when he saw the black plastic garbage bags. The man had thought of everything for him. He opened the other bag and emptied the contents onto his bed. Then he took the bag and suitcase into the bathroom. He also took the plastic bags and began putting the body parts into them.

The head was first. It was easy, like keeping a bowling ball. Next were the arms, legs and thighs. They were wrapped separately in pairs. The torso was quite heavy and required a bit more work. Fortunately, the plastic bag was big enough. He cut the orange T-shirt into strips and used them to tie the package containing the thighs. He cut the blue underwear and used it to secure the bag with the legs. Then he took string from his bag to tie the torso. He put the packages into the man's suitcase and carrier bag, and kept them in the wardrobe. After that, he took a shower and changed his clothes. It had been a couple of hours since he checked into Room 1511 with the man.

He rummaged through the man's belongings and checked the wallet. Inside was a gold credit card, cash and other personal cards. He rubbed away the signatures on the credit card and passport with a thinner-like solution which could erase ink. He then forged his own "Lowe" signatures. He also removed the man's passport photograph and replaced it with his own.

Normally, he would make a photocopy of the passport, with his photograph over that of the owner's. This way, it would appear to others that he was the owner, making it easier for him to use the owner's credit card or traveller's cheques. Should anyone ask him to prove his identity, he would produce the photocopy. Sorry, the passport was left at the hotel, he would say. They would usually be satisfied. In this case, however, he was able to use the South African passport as the identification page did not have plastic lamination. He just took out Lowe's photograph and replaced it with his own. Now he was ready to go out and use the man's credit card.

Sometime after 5 pm that day, he was at Cost Plus, an electronics shop along Scotts Road, adjacent to Orchard Road. He looked around for a while and was served by salesman Danny Teo. He told Danny he wanted to buy two sets of monochrome and two sets of colour notebook computers. He said he wanted to sell the computers in Mexico for a profit to cover his airfare.

Danny was excited; he was already calculating his commission for selling S$8,600 worth of computers. He asked the customer how he would pay for the computers. By credit card, the man replied, but added that he needed time to think about it first. Danny asked how he could get in touch with the man. He did not want to lose contact with this big customer. The man produced his hotel check-in card and Danny copied the particulars on a piece of paper. He wrote "Lowe G." next to the other information.

The killer took dinner at about 9 pm that day. He chose to eat at the River Garden Restaurant in his hotel. He was a bit tired after his trip to Orchard Road and did not want to go anywhere else. He looked at the menu and ordered fillet steak and a glass of white wine. As he ate, he thought about his victim, but that did not bother him. Right now, he was hungry. He also decided to spend the dead man's money the next day.

After dinner, he called his ex-wife, Maria, in Mexico. When a little girl answered, he said, "Hi Lara! It's Daddy." But the girl responded: "My daddy is with me. Who are you?" He was stunned. Who was Maria with and what had she told their daughter? He did not know what to say to Lara. He hung up, then went to a bar and got himself drunk.

When he awoke early the next morning on March 9, he could not find his pouch containing his passport and traveller's cheques. "Damn! Did I drop it somewhere after I got drunk?" he thought. "Now I will have to report the passport and cheques missing." As he took a lift down to the lobby, he remembered his victim. He had to make an excuse for his disappearance, or someone might get suspicious.

It was about 8 am and Tay Yue Mae, a banquet sales executive, was on duty. He told her about the man and how they decided to share a room. He said, "Did he collect his deposit when he checked out last night? I discovered the previous night that he was gay, so I returned his share of the money and sent him packing."

Yue May thought it was unfortunate that such a thing could happen to the soft-spoken, mild-mannered man in front of her. She checked the computer and told him that Lowe had not checked out. He asked her to cancel that name, leaving only his own, Simon James Davis, on the register. He said he might stay for another night and would pay the deposit after he reported his missing documents.

He was at the Thomas Cook office in Anson Road, in the main business district, at about 9.30 am. He told Yvonne Lim, the foreign exchange supervisor, that nine booklets of his traveller's cheques totalling US$8,000 were missing. He said the last time he used the cheques was when he signed US$100 in Hongkong while in transit. He also said he was employed as a shopkeeper by a Mr Scripps in Cancun, Mexico. Yvonne told him that investigations would have to be conducted before he could be given a refund. He left and went to the British High Commission to apply for a replacement passport.

Meanwhile, chambermaid Siti Samiah opened the door to Room 1511. Her duty was to make up the rooms on the 15th floor, and she did not see anything unusual in Room 1511—nothing that would not be found in an ordinary room occupied by guests. The usual signs were there: bedsheet and blanket pulled out, towels used. But in Room 1511, she thought she smelled something strange in the bathroom and near the wardrobe. However, she did not open the wardrobe to see why it stank. She just did what she was paid to do—clean and make up the room. One should not be too nosy.

Sometime after 1.30 pm, the killer was served by teller Tan Suan Kiow at the DBSBank in Raffles City Shopping Centre. He wanted to withdraw S$12,000 from Gerard George Lowe's credit card account and gave the man's card and passport to her. The teller saw that the card and passport both had the same name. The photograph also resembled the man in front of her. She processed the transaction but it was rejected as the approved amount was only S$6,000. He said he would take the $6,000, and the woman gave him six S$1,000 notes. He took the cash and left. It was easy money.

He then went into Sogo Department Store near by and looked around for a pair of shoes as his was getting a bit worn. He decided on a pair of Nike Alpha Trainers, taking size 10 as he was rather big and well-built. He also bought two pairs of socks. The total purchase was S$184.07 and he used the man's credit card to pay for it.

Next, he went to Pertama Raffles City, an electronics shop in the same building. He remembered that his sister would be celebrating her 40th birthday soon, and decided to buy her a gift. He browsed through the store and settled on a model VTH 323 Thomson video recorder. He also chose a pair of Aiwa speakers for himself. He told salesman Kelvin Lee he was from South Africa and had a sister in Britain. He said he wanted to mail the video recorder to her. Kelvin offered to carry the item to the post office on the ground floor but he declined. He used the credit card to pay for both items, costing a total of S$572.

At the post office, he bought plastic "cushion" wrapper and brown paper. He packed the video recorder and paid S$145.50 for postage. On the parcel posting form, he wrote the name of the recipient—Janet Scripps of Hertford, Herts, England.

Despite having killed the South African tourist for his money, he also thought of other ways to instant wealth. He bought five Singapore Sweep lottery tickets, the first prize of which was S$1 million.

When he got back to his hotel room at about 5 pm, his room had been made up. He opened the wardrobe and saw that the two bags containing the body parts were still there. Although he had taken care to seal the bags carefully, there was an unpleasant smell when he opened the wardrobe. The smell of decomposition, it seemed, was penetrating through the bags. He pushed the bags deeper into the wardrobe and, while doing so, noticed his black pouch at a corner. He opened it and saw his traveller's cheques and passport. How careless of him to have dropped it there, he thought. But he smiled as it meant he did not have to wait for replacement traveller's cheques before he could use his money. He would also have a second passport as the new one from the British High Commission would be ready the next day.

There was a message for him: someone had telephoned while he was out. It was the computer salesman, Danny

Teo. When he returned the call, Danny asked whether he had reached a decision regarding the computers. " I called to ask if you'd be interested in buying a fifth computer. It's mine actually but it's brand new and I can sell it to you cheaper. Can I come and see you?" He was a bit reluctant but finally said yes.

Danny was in his room about three hours later, at 8 pm. He saw that the two beds were neatly made. He did not pay attention to the other things in the room and jumped straight into his sales pitch. Danny called the man "Mr Lowe" and persuaded him to buy his notebook computer for a cash payment of S$1,800. He told Danny he did not have much cash but had traveller's cheques instead. Danny said he could cash the cheques at the hotel but the man replied that the hotel did not give good rates. He told Danny he would give his decision the following day.

While in the room, he chatted casually with the salesman. Among other things, he bragged about how easy it was to have two passports just by reporting to the embassy that the first had been lost. Danny was not keen to listen to his rambling. If "Mr Lowe" did not want to buy his computers, he had to look for an excuse to leave. It came when his pager beeped. His friend, Lawrence Quek, was looking for him. After calling Lawrence on the telephone in the room, he told "Mr Lowe" he had to leave.

On the way to the door, Danny passed the bathroom and thought of going in. After all, he had been in the room for slightly over an hour. But he decided against using it and left. The man accompanied Danny down to the lobby and when the salesman was gone, he smiled to himself. Two persons had been inside his room but neither had suspected anything.

The next morning, which was March 10, he approached Tay Yue Mae at the hotel front office again and asked if she knew of any coin shops in Singapore. He said he was interested in buying Mexican gold coins. Yue Mae did not know but asked her colleague, Cheah Chin Shyuan, who wrote the address of a shop in Orchard Road.

At about 10 am, he was at Raffles City Shopping Centre's DBSBank, where teller Tan Suan Kiow attended to him again. He wanted to withdraw S$2,000 from the gold MasterCard. The transaction was approved and he was given two S$1,000 notes. On his way out of the shopping centre, he noticed that the counter in the main atrium was selling tickets to a classical music concert: the Singapore Symphony Orchestra was playing at the Victoria Concert Hall. He used the credit card to buy a $30 ticket.

Chambermaid Siti Samiah entered Room 1511. Once again, she detected the strange smell coming from the bathroom and wardrobe but did not do anything about it. She merely carried on with her work of cleaning the bathroom and tidying the room. If the guest did not complain about the smell, why should she?

Sometime in the afternoon, "Davis" went to the Thomas Cook office in Anson Road. He told Yvonne Lim that he wanted to telegraph some money to a bank account in the

United States, and was given a form to fill. As he was writing, he paused suddenly, trying hard to recall something. He gave up in the end and told Yvonne he had forgotten his own account number. He then left but said he would return the next day.

Since he could not complete the transaction, he thought it might be a good idea to have more money, and went to the DBSBank to withdraw more cash from the credit card. This time, he asked for S$1,000 but only S$400 was approved. He took the money in eight S$50 notes. A total of S$8,400 in cash had been withdrawn from the credit card account.

When he returned to his room later that day, he sensed that the foul smell was getting stronger. Perhaps it was time to change to another hotel. He picked up the telephone directory and went through the list of hotels. He chose the ones on Sentosa, a popular tourist resort. He called both Shangri-La's Rasa Sentosa Resort and The Beaufort Singapore, but found the rates too high—about double what he was paying at the River View. Then he thought of a cheaper solution to his problem. If some of the body parts were thrown away, the smell would perhaps not be so bad. He decided to get rid of the head first.

He carried it in a blue document bag and went to Orchard Road, looking for a place to dump the package. He soon found a big monsoon drain running between Orchard and Somerset Roads, near the Somerset subway station. He walked along the drain and looked around to see if anyone was watching. No one was. He took the package out and threw it into the drain, then strolled away as if nothing had happened. He looked at his watch—it was about 7 pm, and he had a concert to attend.

After 8 pm, he was sitting inside the Victoria Concert Hall, taking in Tchaikovsky and Brahms.

He decided to check out on March 11, three days after he killed the man. He woke up early as he had to get rid of the other body parts as well. At about 6.30 am, he lugged the black suitcase out of his room. It was quite heavy. He took a lift down and carried it across the lobby. Not many people were there then. As the suitcase seemed to grow heavier with each step he took, he put it down at the front porch. He then dragged it towards the river running behind the hotel. There were shrubs along the side of the road which provided cover.

When he reached the river bank, he checked if the coast was clear, then opened the suitcase and emptied the body parts into the river. He also threw the suitcase away. He wiped his hands on his trousers and walked back to his hotel.

He had a light breakfast before checking out. He packed all the man's belongings into his bag; he did not want to throw the things away as he could use them or sell them. He carried his black carrier bag and another bag containing the remaining body parts to the check-out counter. At the counter, he was told that the total amount on his bill was S$760. He was dissatisfied and questioned cashier Julie Seah on the service charges, which he disputed. After she took time to explain the charges to him, he finally settled the bill and left in a huff.

His next destination was the waterfront near Marina Square Shopping Centre, which faced the sea. It was before 10 am and not many people were around as many of the shops did not open before 11 am. He walked to the far end of the shore, which was obscured by trees and bushes. He emptied the body parts in the green-purple-black bag into the sea. He did not throw the bag away as he thought it looked quite new and wanted to keep it, but the smell of death in it gagged him. He thought of a solution.

He walked to the Smart Supermarket on the ground floor of the shopping centre and bought a bottle of Lynx deodorant. That should mask the smell, he thought. He sprayed the deodorant into the bag, then took a cab at the nearby taxi stand and directed the driver to the Thomas Cook office in Anson Road.

He was at the Thomas Cook office at about 11 am. He told foreign exchange supervisor Sara Eng that he wanted to cancel the stop order on his missing traveller's cheques as he had found them. He showed her the cheques and said he wanted to cash them. However, Sara said she needed a day to process the transaction because of the initial stop order. He was unhappy and kicked up a fuss. Manager Ng Hsian Pin was called to explain the problem to him.

In the end, he relented and said he wanted to telegraph the money to his Citibank account in San Francisco instead. He handed over US$5,000 in traveller's cheques and S$8,500 in cash. He also paid S$485 for a Singapore-Bangkok-Phuket-Singapore air ticket. He told them he would return a few days later to check on the cash transfer.

As he was walking out of the office, he opened the green-purple-black bag to place some documents inside. However, he changed his mind quickly as the foul smell was still there; the deodorant could not disguise it. Disgusted, he left the bag on a sofa in the waiting room and left.

Just before 7 pm on March 11, he boarded Thai Airways flight TG 410 and left Singapore for Bangkok.

That same day in South Africa, Vanessa Lowe was distressed as the reliable man whom she had married seemed to have vanished. When she did not receive a call from him on March 8 as promised, she was a bit concerned but assured herself that some legitimate reasons could have prevented him from calling her.

When she still did not hear from him by March 10, she thought, "He said if he did not call today, he would be on the plane and would arrive tomorrow."

So early the next day, she drove to the airport. It was a Saturday morning and the South African Airways flight from Singapore arrived at 6.20 am, but her husband was not on board. She started to get really worried and called his elder sister, Terry. Terry made checks with Lowe's bank and found that his credit card had been used in Singapore. That reassured Vanessa.

One day passed and when there was still no news of him, Terry sought the help of a contact in Singapore to send out a missing person report. It was faxed to all police stations, hospitals and the media in Singapore.

What had happened to Gerard George Lowe?

5

THE KILLER IN PHUKET, THAILAND

It was March 15 and Lowe's killer was on board Thai Airways' flight TG 213 to Phuket, Thailand. He had been in Bangkok for a little over three days without much gain, and his search for a suitable victim did not turn up anything. In the meantime, he had gone to various places and visited the notorious red light district in Patpong, where there were girls and excitement aplenty. The streets and shopping centres of Bangkok also beckoned with all sorts of goods, both fake and genuine, but he was not lured by them. He had something bigger in mind: ways to accquire more money. He would do anything to achieve this objective.

Robbing a bank was too difficult. It required meticulous planning, and he was not very good at this. While in Singapore, he could not even look after his own pouch, which contained his money and passport. He thought he had lost it and made a report. Thanks to himself, he had to make a return trip to Singapore to sort out the mess concerning his "lost" traveller's cheques. His instructions had been to stop the finder from using the cheques. Who would have thought that this person would turn out to be himself, he cursed.

He had also tried drug trafficking but had been caught too many times. The task paid well but only in the short term, and he always ended up broke after serving time in prison. The risk was also very high. These days, law enforcers in the airports were eagle-eyed and well trained. They could tell if one had something to hide. There were also the non-humans who liked to come up close to sniff at him. Stupid dogs; he hated them.

Forgery and fraud involving credit cards and traveller's cheques, on the other hand, were right up his alley. He knew how to erase the signatures on stolen credit cards, forge signatures and tamper with identification documents such as passports and driving licences. He also knew that such crimes had short life spans—they always ended when owners reported their cards or cheques missing. Then he would not be able to use the stolen cards again, unless something stopped the owners from reporting their losses—like when they were dead. That was why he decided to kill.

He chose tourists as his victims because they carried the most cash, credit cards and traveller's cheques. People on holiday usually have so many things to buy—like the man he killed in Singapore a week ago. He got close to S$10,000 for one or two days' work. He picked only Caucasian tourists as he was more familiar with such people, being Caucasian himself. Asians, to him, looked too much alike; sometimes, he could hardly tell one from the other. Besides, what would happen if he picked a local by mistake? A local in trouble would draw the police like flies, and he certainly did not want any attention. He had cut up the body of the South African so that no one could identify him. If no one knew who the victim was, the identity of the killer would also remain a mystery.

His luck in Bangkok, however, had not been so good. He had looked for three days without finding a target. Most tourists travelled in pairs or groups. He liked those who were alone so that he could offer his company—in effect, an offer of death. He decided to make Phuket, a popular island holiday resort in Thailand, his new hunting ground.

Now, seated beside a window on board flight TG 213, he looked at the other passengers as they boarded. The flight was quite full; there were more than 100 passengers heading for Phuket from Bangkok. Most were tourists from overseas, many of them Caucasians. He stared at them as they looked for their seats, but no one sat next to him. He later noticed a petite, bespectacled middle-aged woman boarding the plane. She was accompanied by a boyish-looking young man—probably her son, he thought. He noticed that the youth had a cement cast on one of his legs—possibly the result of a fracture. That made him an easy target. He paid special attention to these two people, seated two rows in front of him. They travelled as a pair but somehow looked vulnerable. He had found his victims.

Canadian Sheila Damude was very close to her only child, Darin. Since her husband died many years ago, Darin had been her main source of comfort. She also kept close contact with her sister, Karin Clarke, and good friend, Maja Briscoe. She was 49 but looked much younger with her blonde hair and steel-rimmed spectacles. She worked as an administrator in a school in British Columbia, Canada. Darin, her 23-year-old son, was a college student—handsome, dark-haired and fashionable, with an earring in his left ear. He had inherited his good looks from his dad. His mother was his best friend and confidante.

When his college break began in February, he saw it as an opportunity to travel overseas for a long holiday. He persuaded his mother to take leave so that they could go together. Both were well-travelled and had visited many Western countries. This time, they wanted to see countries in Asia; among their choice destinations were Thailand, Japan and Hongkong. They planned to be away for a few weeks.

They arrived in Bangkok on March 12, checked into the Siam City Hotel and explored the city for three days. They visited crocodile farms, various temples and also the famous floating market, touted as the Venice of the East. On March 15, they flew to Phuket, hoping to relax by the Patong seaside, away from the maddening traffic crawl in the city.

Flight TG 213 touched down in Phuket at about 4 pm. The Damudes alighted and followed signs leading them to the baggage claim area. Sheila carried a floral bag with rose prints while Darin lugged a big green backpack. They headed for the limousine counter to hire a car to take them to the hotel. While they were talking to the clerk, a tall and friendly-looking man greeted them. "Hi. My name is Simon Davis. How are you?"

After the Canadians introduced themselves, the man said he was also touring Phuket and had been on the same flight as them. He asked which hotel they would be staying in. Sheila said they had not decided but would probably settle on Neptuna Hotel. He suggested travelling together to keep each other company. He also asked if they would mind sharing a cab and suggested that it would be a good idea for them to stay at the same hotel. The Damudes were friendly and hospitable by nature and saw nothing wrong with such an arrangement. Besides, the soft-spoken man looked very decent. They invited him to join them so he smiled, picked up his black carrier bag and followed them to a waiting cab.

Cabby Weerasak Wongpanich was waiting inside his white Toyota Corona at a nearby car park when an employee from the limousine counter brought the Damudes and the man to him. He helped them put their luggage into the boot of his car. Darin then slowly lowered himself and his leg cast into the front seat next to the driver, while his mother and the man sat behind. When Sheila instructed the driver to go to Neptuna Hotel, he asked if they had already made reservations there. Her reply was "no". Sensing an opportunity to earn some easy money, Weerasak persuaded them to stay at the Nilly's Marina Inn instead. This hotel, he said, was popular with tourists as it was located next to Patong beach. As the Caucasians had no objection, Weerasak was soon driving cheerfully towards Nilly's Marina Inn located along Thaweephong Road, next to the beach.

During the journey, Sheila, being her usual chatty self, initiated most of the conversation. She got the man, whom she had met a little while ago, talking about himself. She found out that he was from Britain but had a wife and daughter in Mexico. Apart from taking a short vacation, he was in Thailand to buy clothes for his shop, he said. While the two were talking at the back, Darin sat quietly in front, enjoying the passing scenery. He looked back occasionally and smiled when he saw his mother talking to the man. Mum sure had a way with people, he thought.

They reached Nilly's Marina Inn shortly before 5 pm. Weerasak got out to help his passengers take their luggage out of the boot. He also helped Sheila carry her bag into the hotel. Strictly speaking, this was not part of his duties but he wanted to go into the hotel too. He had a small "commission" waiting for him for taking guests to the hotel. That was one of the perks of being an airport cabby. Hotels were willing to give such incentives to cab drivers to help bring in a steady stream of guests. On this occasion, Weerasak had an unexpected bonus as Sheila tipped him as well for being so helpful.

Oy LoGate was on duty when the Canadians and Briton approached the front desk. She greeted them with a *"Sawadee-kah"* and asked for their passports to check them in. While noting their particulars, she wrote the name of the man who was with the Damudes as "Simon Davis, Canadian." The man carried a British passport but Oy made a mistake concerning his nationality. She thought all three were travelling together as a group. It seemed that way to her because she saw them talking and laughing among themselves at the counter. Before the new guests were given their keys, they were taken to view the rooms as they had insisted on choosing for themselves. In the end, the Canadians decided on Room 43 while the man chose Room 48.

For some strange reason, Room 48 was next to Room 43. The rooms were not located in numerical order and the hotel might have a reason for this, but "Davis" did not need to know. He was happy with the arrangement and pleased that he had chosen a room next to the Canadians. This made it easier for him to approach them.

After getting their keys from the reception counter, they returned to their rooms together. Before Sheila entered Room 43 with her son, she asked the "nice man" what he would be doing for the rest of the evening. "Why not join us for dinner?" she suggested. He replied that he was tired and would probably remain in his room and call for room service. He thanked her for the offer and suggested meeting for breakfast instead. "I will knock on your door at about 8 am tomorrow," he said. "Okay," was Sheila's reply.

Before she went into her room, she said goodnight to the man and saw him smiling at her. Perhaps it was the dim corridor lights ... apart from the smile, she did not notice anything unusual.

That night, Sheila and Darin had dinner at the hotel coffee house. Mother and son talked about what they would do the next day and discussed their plans to visit

Phi Phi Island. They also talked about the man they had met earlier at the airport. Sheila said it was quite unusual for a 1.9-m tall and rather muscular-looking man to be so gentle. His voice was so soft at times that she could hardly hear him.

While the Damudes were enjoying their dinner, the man was hard at work. He had lied when he said he was tired and wanted to remain in his room. He did this because he did not want to be with them; he had more important things to do—like preparing for their deaths.

He was already out of his room a short while after he said goodnight to the Canadians. He left the hotel with a clear idea of where he wanted to go. It was getting dark and he could see various stalls being set up by the road for the night market, one of the main attractions for tourists in Phuket. After a day of swimming or playing on the beach, it would be fun to browse through the stalls which sold clothes and souvenirs. But he was not interested in buying and only wanted to look for a motorcycle rental stall. There were a few of them in Phuket as the locals knew it was a good way to cash in on tourists who wanted to explore the place on their own. He did not have to walk far as there was a vehicle rental stall near the hotel.

He rented a motorcycle for two days as he figured he would need that much time to finish the job he had in mind if he worked fast. He had taken about three days to complete the task in Singapore. After paying the stall owner, he mounted the bike and rode off. He had been to Phuket before and although he was not very familiar with the roads, he recognised certain stretches. He travelled north and soon passed the Patong business district on his way to Kathu district. Riding past the Kathu police station, he came to a bridge along the Sahm-gorng Road, where he stopped to look around. He was about 9 km from his hotel. From the bridge, he could see the river and a small path which led to a disused mine. He liked the place. He told himself he would be back and rode off.

On the way back to Nilly's Marina Inn, he thought he would do some sightseeing. He stopped by the beach, sat on the sand and enjoyed the breeze. He looked around and saw many other tourists, but they were all in groups and did not interest him.

Less than half an hour later, he was back on his bike. He wanted to take a look at the Coral Beach Hotel along Thaweephong Road, a short distance south of his own hotel. He thought about changing hotels after completing the next day's task. Later, as he rode back towards Nilly's Marina Inn, he noticed thick undergrowth and bushes along the road; the whole area was dark and quiet. It was perfect for what he planned to do.

It was about 9 pm by the time he walked back to his room. As he opened the door, he noticed that the light was on in Room 43; the Damudes were in. He went into his room and closed the door quietly. He did not want them to know he had been out. After taking a shower, he unzipped his black carrier bag and took out his tools: the hammer, electrical stun device, knives, handcuffs and a can of mace. He laid the items on his bed and examined each one carefully.

He picked up the stun device and pressed the trigger button. Small electrical sparks flew from the two pointed tips, accompanied by an "ack-ack" sound. The battery was still good. The Z-Force III device could give out a 40,000-volt charge, enough to immobilise a man or even leave him unconscious. If it was applied on sensitive parts of the body, such as the eyes, there would be graver consequences. Despite the high voltage it could generate, the device worked with only a nine-volt battery, thanks to its complex circuitry.

He also had a can of mace which could blind a person temporarily if it was sprayed in the eyes. But he had hardly used it since he bought it in the United States before flying to Singapore. He picked up one of the knives, a metallic Police brand foldable knife. The blade was about the length of his palm, its top slightly curved. The edge was serrated, like a small saw, and ended in a very sharp point. It had the features of the perfect deboning knife for a butcher. It was also a lethal weapon for a killer. He took out an oilstone from a small pouch and sharpened the knife with it. After that, he tested his handcuffs to make sure they snapped on tightly and quickly. He then held up his hammer and swung it in the air several times. It weighed 1.5 kg and had a hardwood handle and a red metal head with flat surfaces on both sides. He smiled as he looked at the hammer, which had served him well in Singapore. He would use it again here ...

He took out a small bag and put his weapons into it. He did not want the Canadians to see them—until it was time for them to die. He put the bag aside and laid on his bed, hoping to catch some sleep. He was ready for a long day ahead.

The Damudes woke up slightly after 7 am on March 16. They started the day early as they had booked a day tour to Phi Phi Island. Also, they were supposed to have breakfast with Davis. He would come knocking on the door soon. Sheila and Darin took turns to go to the bathroom. Darin took slightly longer because it was troublesome to use the toilet bowl with one of his legs in a cement cast. But both of them were ready by 8 am.

Their doorbell rang a short while after. When Sheila opened the door, she saw the friendly and soft-spoken Davis holding a small carrier bag. He smiled broadly and they exchanged greetings. At the same time, she turned to indicate to Darin that they were ready to leave for breakfast. Darin was seated at the balcony of the room, which had a good view of the beach. Just as he was about to get up, the tall Briton walked into the room and said they were lucky to occupy a room with a scenic view. He could not even see the sea from his room. He walked towards the balcony and pretended to look at the sea. From the corner of his eye, he was actually watching Darin and Sheila closely. He put one of his hands into the pocket of his trousers and clutched the stun device tightly.

The moment Darin turned around to talk to his mother, he acted swiftly, whipping out the stun gun and jabbing it at the young man's neck. The powerful shock jolted Darin and sent him reeling. The whole thing was too sudden for Sheila. She screamed as her son slumped onto the floor.

He quickly produced his knife from his bag, knelt down and arm-locked the semi-conscious Darin. He hissed at Sheila to shut up, or he would hurt her son. He also ordered her to close the door. Sheila did as she was told as she had no choice—the man had placed his knife against Darin's neck. She could see that her son was slowly regaining his composure but was still weak. What was happening? Who was this man? Why was he hurting Darin?

He told Sheila that he only wanted money and would not harm her son if she obeyed his instructions. She could only nod her head as she was terrified and her body was trembling. When he said he wanted all their money and valuables, she ran to fetch her handbag.

While she was searching her handbag for money, the man pushed Darin against the floor. He took out his handcuffs and clamped them on the young man's wrists, then relaxed a little when he was in total control. Sheila threw her money on the bed—about $1,000 Canadian dollars in all. He took a quick look and said, "Where are your credit cards and traveller's cheques?" She handed over US$1,600 worth of traveller's cheques from the Royal Bank of Canada and two gold Visa credit cards. One of the cards belonged to Darin.

He took the cards, put them on the bed and said to Sheila, "I want you to write a letter saying that you authorise your son to use your credit card and traveller's cheques. You will sign your name at the end of the letter." Sheila went to the table, sat down, picked up the pen and started scribbling. She did not understand the implication of what she was doing; the only thing that mattered was the safety of her son.

When she finished writing the letter, he gave another instruction. She was to go down to the hotel reception and tell the staff that she and her son would check out of Room 43 in the afternoon. Sheila wanted to know why. He said he wanted them to leave Phuket, or he would kill them. Sheila said she would do as he said as long as Darin was not harmed. She then grabbed her room key and dashed out of the room.

Oy LoGate was on duty at the reception counter when Sheila came rushing towards her. Oy recognised the friendly Canadian woman—only this time, she behaved differently. She spoke curtly and appeared to be in distress. She told Oy that she wanted to check out later that day. The receptionist said it would take only a while to process the request and handed her a check-out slip to sign. After that, she turned around to get the room registration card from a cabinet behind her. When she turned back a few seconds later, the guest was no longer there, but had left her room key at the counter.

Sheila did not know she would not see Darin alive again. The moment she stepped out, the man took the red hammer from his bag. Darin could see death beckoning. He struggled to free his arms, which had been secured behind him, but the handcuffs refused to budge. He yelled for help. The man lifted the hammer over his head and swung it with full force at Darin's face. Thack! Blood flew in all directions and splattered onto the glass door, wall, carpet and bed. The blow caused a gaping wound on the right side of the victim's face. Part of his right eye was crushed and sank into the socket. He died instantly.

By the time Sheila returned to the room, the killer was ready for her. He was standing behind the door when she entered. He slammed the door shut and pushed her forward. She fell headlong and landed near the door of the bathroom. He sprang on top of her to press her down, raised his hammer and swung it against the top left part of her head. Thack! The sound of a skull cracking was all too familiar to him. He had completed the task.

He dragged the bodies of mother and son into the bathroom and stripped them naked before proceeding to dismember them. He started with the youth, lifting the body and dropping it into the bathtub. He wielded his sharp knife and plunged it into the neck, as he had done with his South African victim in Singapore. He twisted the blade slowly as he cut into the cervical bones and around the trunk of the neck. The head came off in less than two minutes. The arms were next, followed by the legs. In about half an hour, Darin Damude was no more and his mother was next.

The killer found that he was able to work faster. Practice had made him better at the task and he was able to cut up the woman's body in just over 25 minutes. The butchering was over. He folded his knife and admired his work. There were two heads, two torsos, four arms, four thighs and four legs in the bathtub. Blood was everywhere.

He turned on the shower and splashed water to wash the blood away. He waited for the blood in the body parts to drain away, then picked them up one by one to wash under running water. It did not bother him at all; the parts were like slabs of beef. Not long ago, he had been cutting up cattle and chicken every day for six months—more than 1,000 hours in all. He was used to the sight of body parts and the coppery smell of blood.

However, disposing of the body parts would pose more of a problem as there were twice as many parts as in Singapore. Luckily, he was prepared. He washed himself, then went to his room to fetch some plastic bags. His experience in Singapore had taught him that such bags were very useful, so he had bought some while in Thailand. But he had miscalculated—there were too many parts to wrap this time. There was also no big suitcase to put them in. The woman had a floral carrier bag while her son had a green backpack but both were unsuitable. Boxes would be a better idea and he would have to get one or two. But first, he needed to make sure that no one would suspect anything. He put the parts aside in the bathroom and went down to the reception counter.

He approach Oy calmly and asked if the Canadians had checked out. She said Sheila had returned the key but she did not know whether the guests had left. He told her he believed they had left because there was no answer when he knocked on their door. He then said he wanted to move into their room as his room did not have a sea view. It was about 11 am on March 16 when Oy processed his request.

After he moved from Room 48 to Room 43, he planned

to go out to dispose of the body parts. He knew he had to act fast as he did not have the proper bags to store them in. He carried a small package containing the two heads and some underwear belonging to Sheila. He did not have any use for a woman's undergarments and wanted to throw them away. Before he left the room, he placed a "Please Do Not Disturb" sign outside his door. That would prevent anyone, including the chambermaids, from entering his room.

He walked out with the package. No one paid him any attention as he walked through the lobby to the car park. He mounted his rented motorcycle and headed north. It took about 20 minutes to reach the disused mine at Kathu. He followed a small path to the mine, then dug a shallow grave in the sand. After making sure no one else was around, he opened the package and dropped the two heads and underwear into the hole, then covered them with sand before returning to his motorcycle. On the way back to the hotel, he managed to get two large boxes from a nearby store.

Back in Room 43, he had a lot of work to do. He had to clean the blood splatters in the room. There was blood on the wall, bedsheet, glass door and carpet. It was too bad he could not kill them in the bathroom. He used a piece of cloth to wipe off the blood in the room. He splashed soap and water onto the carpet and tried scrubbing, but some of the stains would not go away. He hoped no one would notice them.

He was able to pack the remaining body parts into the two boxes and thought of disposing them at one go. He could stack the boxes behind him on the motorcycle, but that would be too risky. What if one of the boxes toppled over and the contents spilled out? The consequences would be unthinkable. It would be better to make an extra trip than expose himself to such a risk.

As he carried the big box through the hotel lobby, a bellhop asked whether he needed any help. He smiled and declined. After placing the box on his motorcycle, he set off and travelled south from his hotel. He headed towards Bahn Nai Trang Road, about a kilometre away. He liked the place as there was jungle on both sides. Five minutes later, he stopped by the right side of the road, got off his bike, carried the box and went into the bushes. When he had found a spot well-covered by thick undergrowth, he opened the box and threw the parts among the bushes. He also discarded the box.

He returned to his room for the other box and repeated the process. By the time he finished, it was late afternoon. He sat down in a restaurant and had his first meal of the day.

Back in Room 43 later, he emptied the Canadians' bags and spread their contents on the beds. They were mainly clothes but he was looking for something else. He had already taken their cash, credit cards and traveller's cheques and was now after their personal documents. He went through the woman's handbag and her son's wallet. He took their passports and the youth's driving licence, then sat at the table and proceeded with his work.

He took out his pouch which contained, among other

things, his passport-sized photographs and a stick of glue he had bought in Mexico. On opening the Canadians' passports, he found that he could not remove their photographs as the pages had been laminated in plastic. So he did the next best thing and used the glue to paste his photographs over theirs. The improvised job did not matter as he did not plan to show the passports to any bank teller. All he needed was to make photocopies of the pages. Anyone who saw the photocopies would think he was the person in the passport.

However, he needed to make other changes to the passports too. First, he cut out a small piece of paper, wrote the letter "M" and glued it over the "F" on the data page of Sheila's passport where sex was indicated. Anyone would be crazy to think he would forgo the opportunity to use Sheila's credit card just because she was a woman. Sheila might be too sissy a name for a man but he reckoned that some Asians in this part of the world might not be aware of it. After all, some Thai girls had difficulty pronouncing his name, let alone read English.

As for Darin's passport, he had a different problem. Darin was only 23 while he was 35. A person looking at the year of birth in the passport might think he looked too old to be 23. He cut a small piece of paper, wrote the digit "6" and pasted it on the "7" in the date of birth, changing the year from 1972 to 1962. Darin Damude had aged 10 years instantly to become 33 years old. He whistled cheerfully as he did the same thing to Darin's driving licence.

Later that night, he practised the signatures of Sheila and Darin Damude on his memo pad. He used tracing paper to familiarise himself with the strokes first. It was a bit tedious but he did not mind because every correct stroke meant more cash added to his pocket.

He decided to take a break the next day, on March 17, for he had worked very hard the previous day. He planned to join a day tour and enjoy himself. He selected the tour to Phang-Nga Island, otherwise known as James Bond Island. The island got its nickname because one of the Bond movies, *The Man with the Golden Gun* starring Roger Moore as British secret agent 007, had been filmed there.

He returned to his hotel after the day trip and the following day passed uneventfully. He decided to leave Phuket and return to Singapore as he had unfinished business to settle there. He wanted to make sure that his money and the South African man's money had been properly sent to his Citibank account in San Francisco. The account was not opened under the name of Simon Davis. The name of the account holder was John Martin.

Before he checked out of Nilly's Marina Inn on the morning of March 19, he packed all the Canadians' belongings into the green backpack. He then folded Sheila's floral bag and stuffed it into his own black carrier bag. He did not want to carry so many bags, neither did he want to throw Sheila's bag away as it was still in good condition.

At about 3 pm the same day, a local walking along Sahmgorng Road in Kathu district was drawn to the disused tin mine by dogs barking. He lived close by and was familiar with the surroundings. He walked towards the mine and saw his brown mongrel scraping at something in the sand. He drew nearer and froze in horror when he saw a human head. He ran to the nearest telephone to call the police.

Police Major Anuruth Am-arb was on duty in the Kathu Police Station when one of his officers informed him that someone had found a human head in the disused tin mine. He arrived at the scene shortly before 4 pm, searched the area and found that there were two heads, and not just one. They were lying exposed about 50 m apart. He saw that the flesh had decomposed badly and the human features had rotted away. There was dark and blonde hair scattered in the sand, and silky underwear as well. Major Am-arb removed the heads and hair from the scene and took the specimens to the Vachira Hospital mortuary in Yaowarat Road, Phuket.

The killer boarded a Thai Airways flight to Singapore in the evening. During the journey, he took out the Canadians' passports to look at them. Later, he wrote on one of his Singapore lottery tickets calculations of how much money he had made from the killings. He had about US$30,000 with him before his arrival in Singapore. Then he got about US$10,000 from the South African. He had not had the chance to use the Canadians' credit cards and traveller's cheques yet. Perhaps he would do so in Singapore. He might also find another victim there.

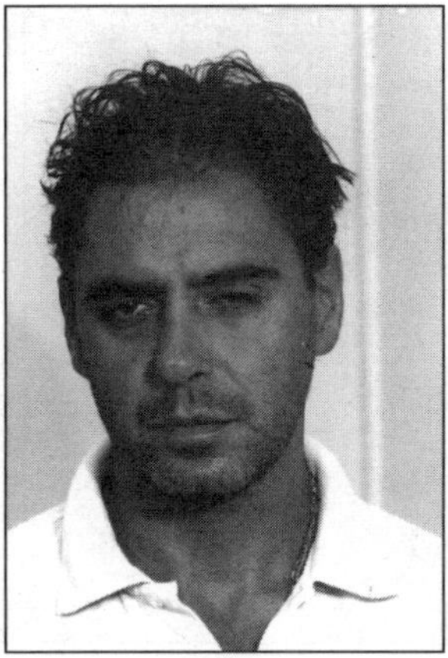

Serial killer John Martin, who murdered a tourist in Singapore and two others in Thailand.

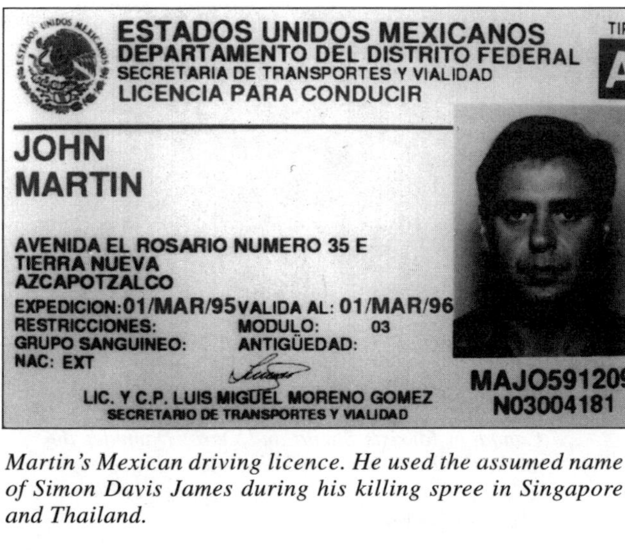

Martin's Mexican driving licence. He used the assumed name of Simon Davis James during his killing spree in Singapore and Thailand.

South African tourist Gerard George Lowe was killed and his body cut up after he shared a hotel room in Singapore with Martin.

Canadian tourists Sheila and Darin Damude: the mother and son pair were killed and their bodies cut up after they checked into the same hotel in Phuket, Thailand, as Martin.

The author (second from left) with "body parts" police investigators (left to right) Assistant Superintendent Gerald Lim, Inspector Zainudin Lee and Staff Sergeant Zainal Abidin.

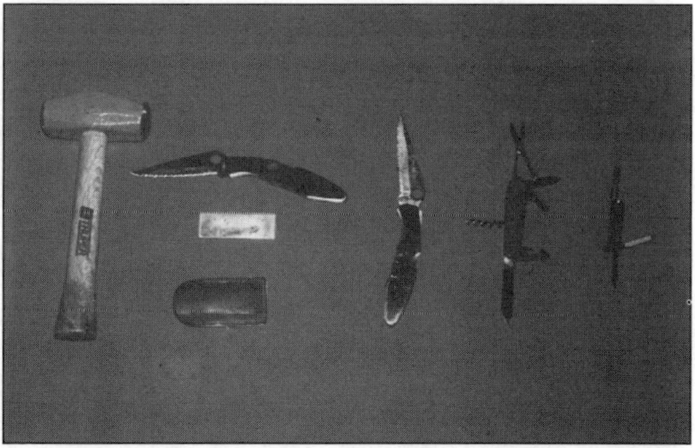

Tools of a killer: the 1.5 kg hammer was used by Martin to bludgeon the head of his victims, and the two serrated knives to slice through body joints. There was even an oilstone to sharpen the knives. The Swiss army knives may not have been used to cut up the bodies.

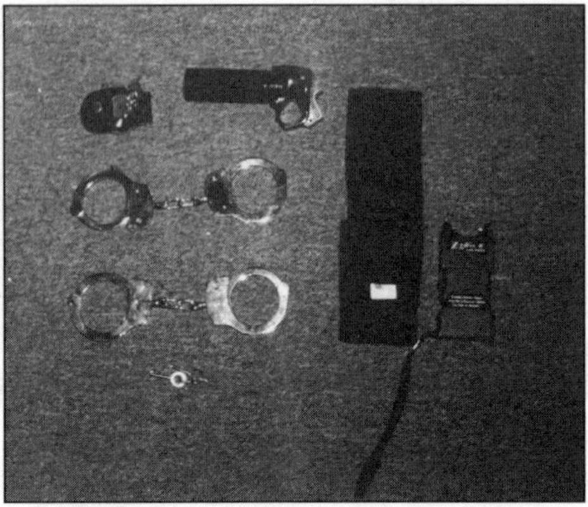

The thumbcuffs, handcuffs and Z-Force III electrical stun device used by Martin to immobilise and restrain his victims.

Part of Martin's loot: the clothes belonging to Sheila Damude.

The River View Hotel, with the Singapore River running behind it. Martin threw some of the body parts into the river, which flows into the sea off Clifford Pier.

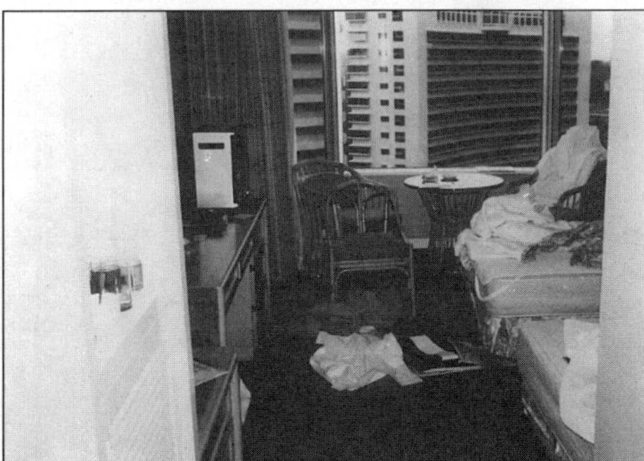

Room 1511 of the River View Hotel: Martin and his South African victim stayed in this room.

Police did not find any blood in the room. The two spots on the floor are solution marks made by the Kestle Meyer test, used by police to detect blood. The test result was negative.

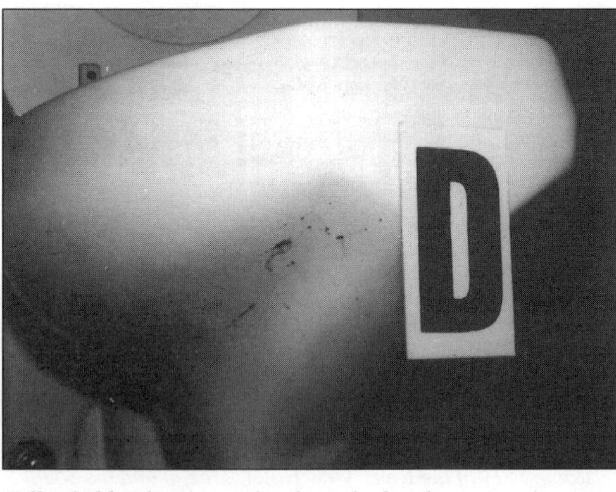

Tell-tale blood stains under the toilet bowl.

The sea off Clifford Pier, where plastic bags containing Lowe's body parts were found.

Bag containing the pair of legs, recovered on March 13, 1995. Similar bags containing the thighs and torso were recovered three days later.

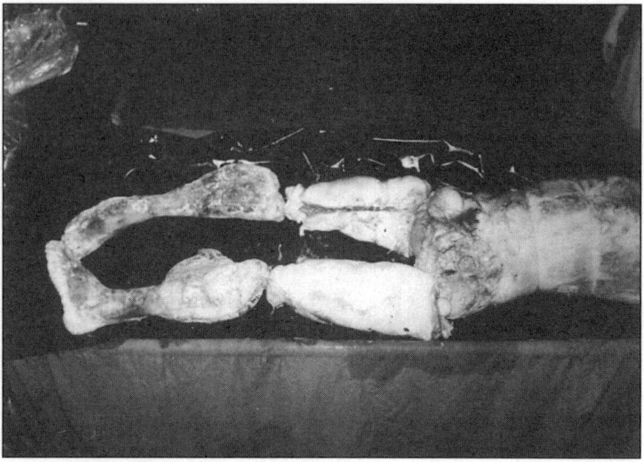

The body parts, cut at the joints, were placed together at the Singapore General Hospital mortuary.

Nilly's Marina Inn in Phuket, Thailand, where the Damudes stayed. Martin occupied the room next to theirs.

The disused tin mine in Kathu district, Phuket, where the skulls of the Damudes were found.

Body parts belonging to Sheila and Darin Damude, tagged for identification purposes.

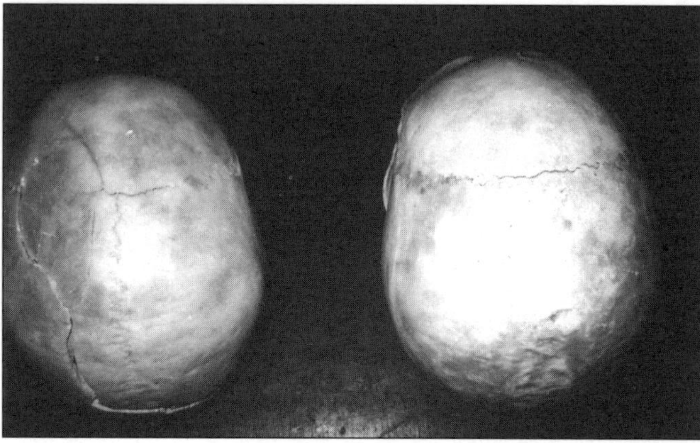

Skulls belonging to the Damudes: Sheila's skull (left) had a serious fracture which ran from the top left portion to the base.

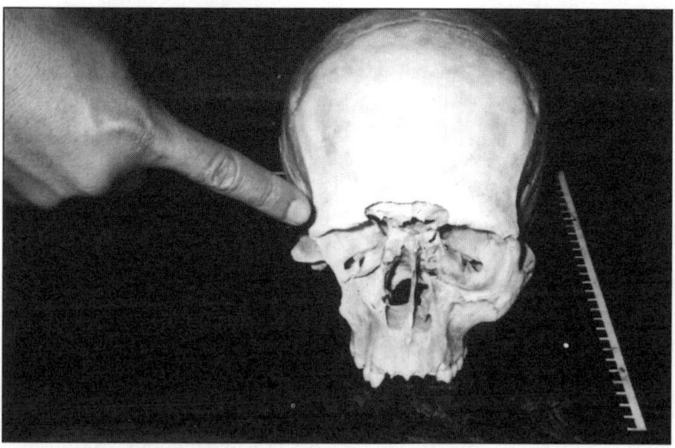

Darin's skull had a serious fracture on the right frontal portion.

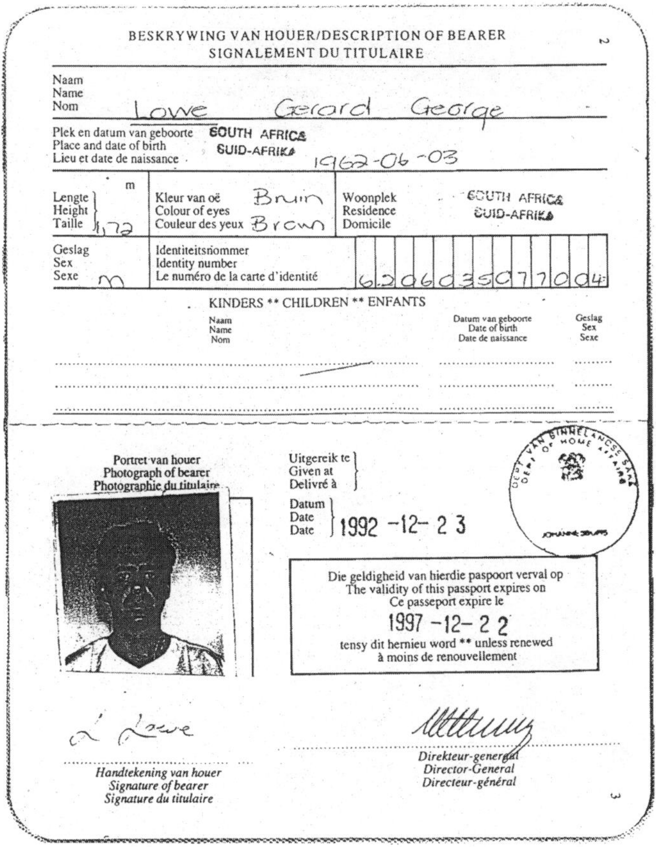

BESKRYWING VAN HOUER/DESCRIPTION OF BEARER
SIGNALEMENT DU TITULAIRE 2

Naam
Name
Nom Lowe Gerard George

Plek en datum van geboorte
Place and date of birth
Lieu et date de naissance SOUTH AFRICA SUID-AFRIKA 1962-06-03

Lengte / Height / Taille (m)	Kleur van oë / Colour of eyes / Couleur des yeux	Woonplek / Residence / Domicile
1,72	Bruin / Brown	SOUTH AFRICA SUID-AFRIKA

Geslag / Sex / Sexe	Identiteitsnommer / Identity number / Le numéro de la carte d'identité
m	6206035077004

KINDERS ** CHILDREN ** ENFANTS

Naam / Name / Nom	Datum van geboorte / Date of birth / Date de naissance	Geslag / Sex / Sexe

Portret van houer
Photograph of bearer
Photographie du titulaire

Uitgereik te / Given at / Delivré à

Datum / Date / Date 1992 -12- 2 3

DEPT VAN BINNELANDSE SAKE / DEPT OF HOME AFFAIRS

Die geldigheid van hierdie paspoort verval op
The validity of this passport expires on
Ce passeport expire le
1997 -12- 2 2
tensy dit hernieu word ** unless renewed
à moins de renouvellement

Handtekening van houer
Signature of bearer
Signature du titulaire

Direkteur-generaal
Director-General
Directeur-général 3

Lowe's passport had Martin's photograph on it.

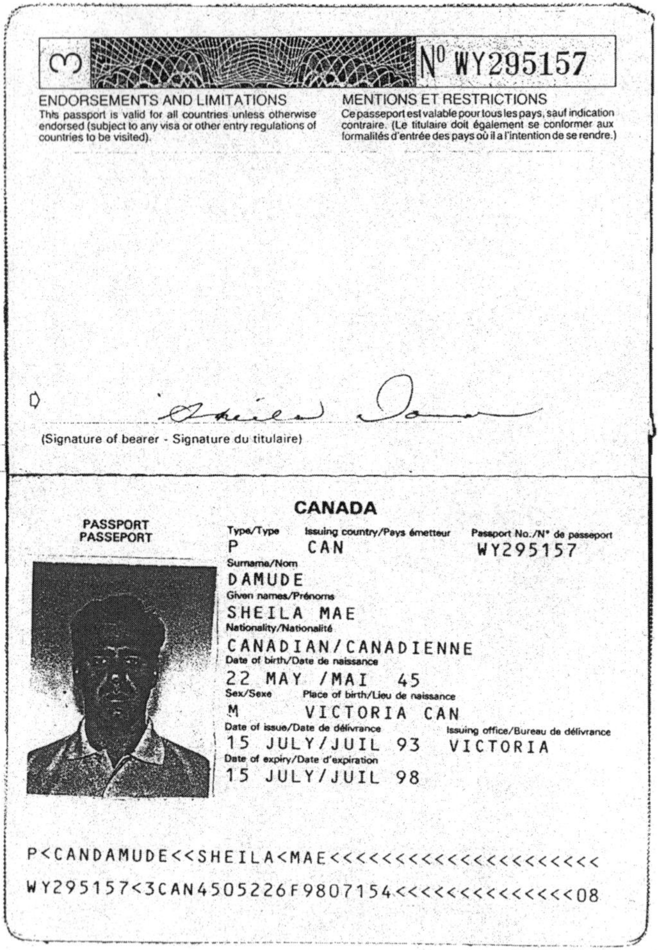

N⁰ WY295157

ENDORSEMENTS AND LIMITATIONS
This passport is valid for all countries unless otherwise endorsed (subject to any visa or other entry regulations of countries to be visited).

MENTIONS ET RESTRICTIONS
Ce passeport est valable pour tous les pays, sauf indication contraire. (Le titulaire doit également se conformer aux formalités d'entrée des pays où il a l'intention de se rendre.)

(Signature of bearer - Signature du titulaire)

CANADA

PASSPORT
PASSEPORT

Type/Type: P
Issuing country/Pays émetteur: CAN
Passport No./N° de passeport: WY295157
Surname/Nom: DAMUDE
Given names/Prénoms: SHEILA MAE
Nationality/Nationalité: CANADIAN/CANADIENNE
Date of birth/Date de naissance: 22 MAY /MAI 45
Sex/Sexe: M
Place of birth/Lieu de naissance: VICTORIA CAN
Date of issue/Date de délivrance: 15 JULY/JUIL 93
Issuing office/Bureau de délivrance: VICTORIA
Date of expiry/Date d'expiration: 15 JULY/JUIL 98

P<CANDAMUDE<<SHEILA<MAE<<<<<<<<<<<<<<<<<<<<<

WY295157<3CAN4505226F9807154<<<<<<<<<<<<<<08

Sheila Damude's passport had Martin's photograph on it. "Sex" had been altered from "F" to "M".

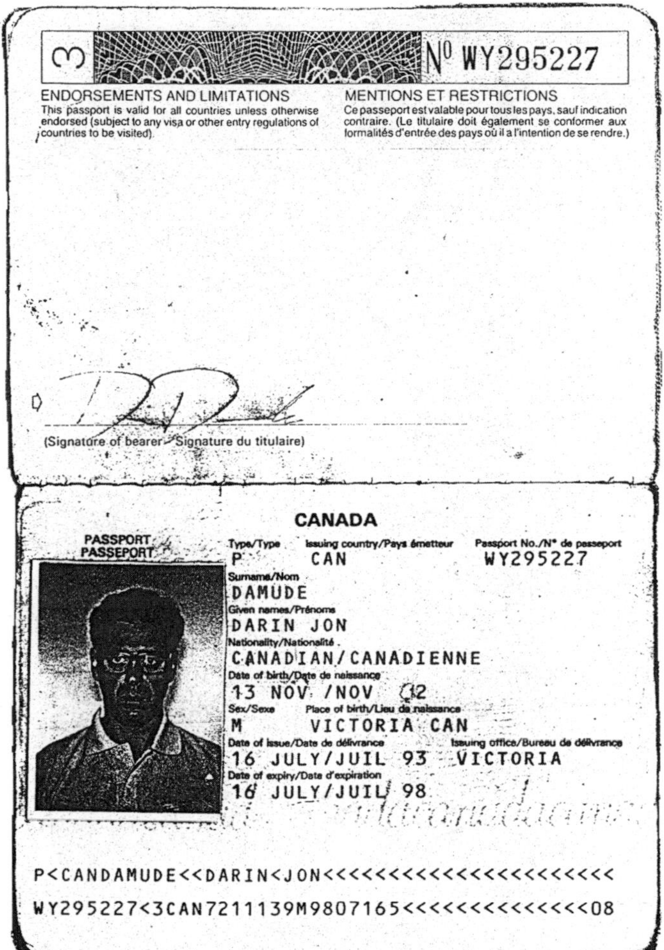

3 Nº WY295227

ENDORSEMENTS AND LIMITATIONS
This passport is valid for all countries unless otherwise endorsed (subject to any visa or other entry regulations of countries to be visited).

MENTIONS ET RESTRICTIONS
Ce passeport est valable pour tous les pays, sauf indication contraire. (Le titulaire doit également se conformer aux formalités d'entrée des pays où il a l'intention de se rendre.)

(Signature of bearer/Signature du titulaire)

CANADA

PASSPORT
PASSEPORT

Type/Type: P
Issuing country/Pays émetteur: CAN
Passport No./N° de passeport: WY295227
Surname/Nom: DAMUDE
Given names/Prénoms: DARIN JON
Nationality/Nationalité: CANADIAN/CANADIENNE
Date of birth/Date de naissance: 13 NOV /NOV 72
Sex/Sexe: M
Place of birth/Lieu de naissance: VICTORIA CAN
Date of issue/Date de délivrance: 16 JULY/JUIL 93
Issuing office/Bureau de délivrance: VICTORIA
Date of expiry/Date d'expiration: 16 JULY/JUIL 98

P<CANDAMUDE<<DARIN<JON<<<<<<<<<<<<<<<<<<<<<<<<<<

WY295227<3CAN7211139M9807165<<<<<<<<<<<<<<08

Darin Damude's passport with Martin's photograph on it.

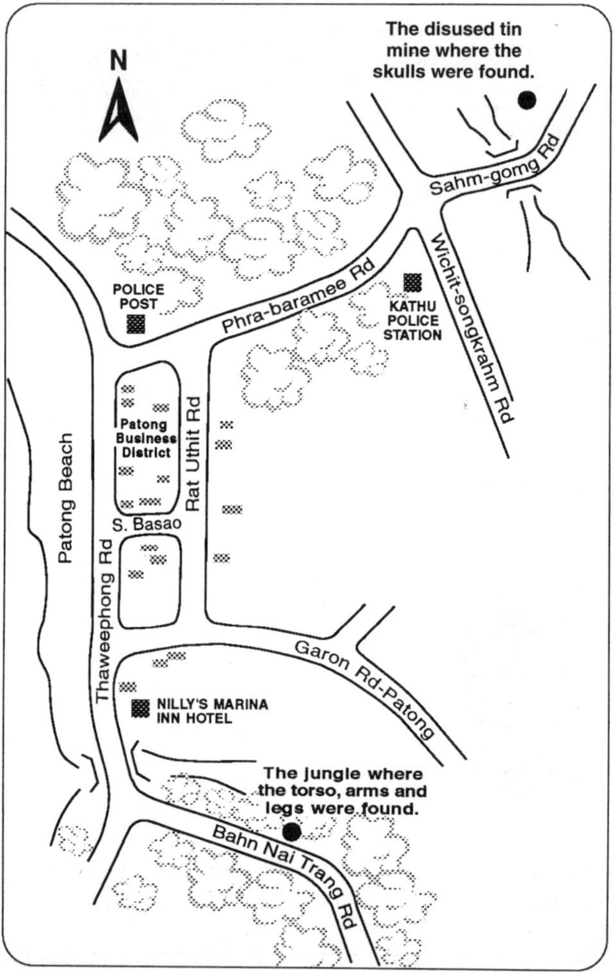

Map showing the places in Phuket, Thailand, where Martin had dumped the Canadians' body parts.

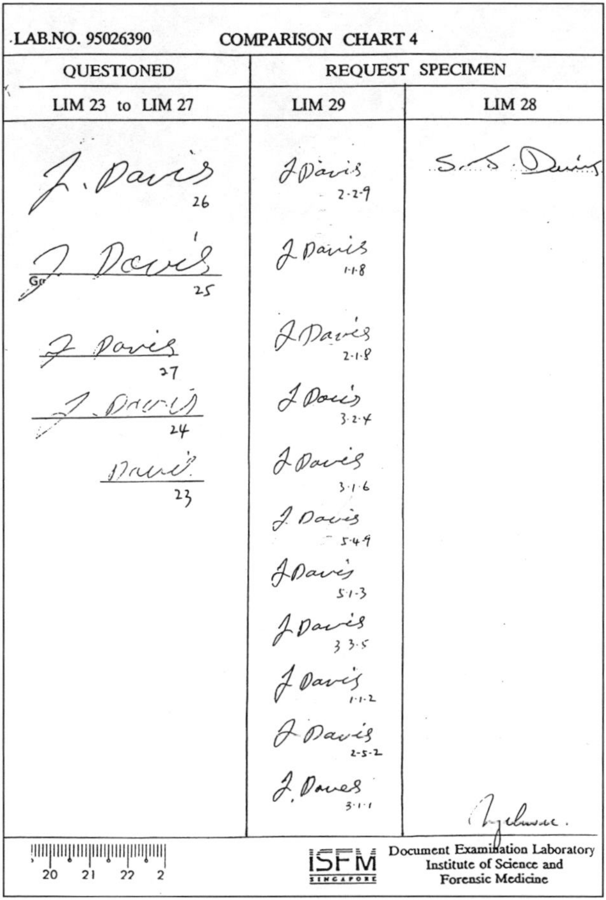

Signature comparison charts: Signatures 23 and 28 were taken from various documents signed by Martin. Signature 23, in particular, was retrieved from the restaurant bill that he signed on the night of March 8. The column "LIM 29" contains specimens obtained from him in prison. A handwriting expert said there were significant similarities in all the signatures.

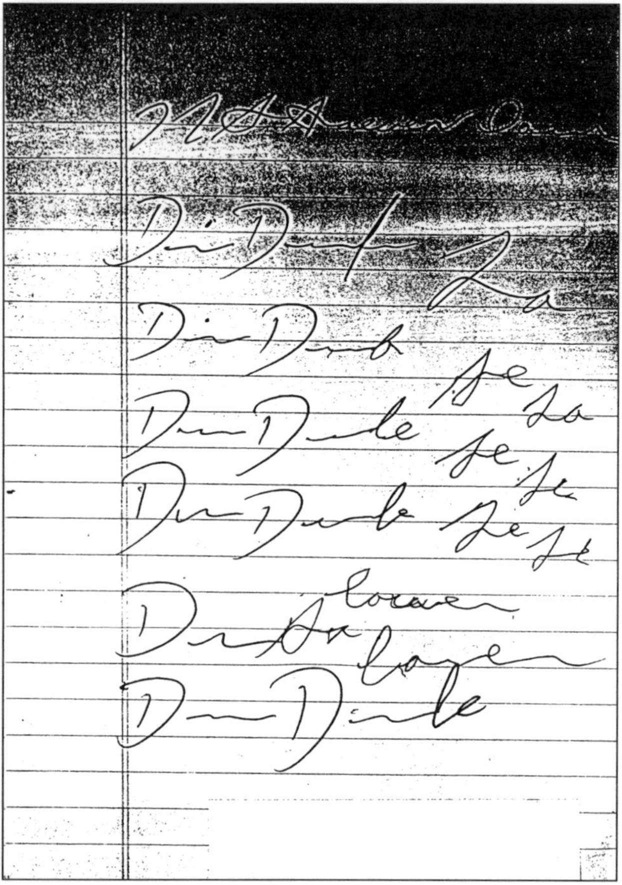

Martin practised Darin Damude's signature on a notepad after he killed the Canadians in their hotel room in Phuket.

6

ARREST IN SINGAPORE

The Thai Airways flight from Phuket touched down at Singapore's Changi International Airport after 8 pm on March 19. The man was anxious to check into a hotel quickly as he was tired. He headed towards the Immigration counter and baggage claims section. He had checked in his black carrier bag and the green backpack as he did not want to lug them around. The bags were quite heavy with his belongings and those of his victims.

He queued for about 15 minutes at the Immigration counter, then gave his British passport to the woman officer. She keyed in his name, Simon Davis, and waited for the computer to respond. A short while later, a message flashed on her screen and caused her heart to miss a beat. The message told her that the man before her was wanted by the police. She fought to remain calm while she secretly alerted the control room for help. To buy time, she smiled weakly and told the man to wait for a while as the system was rather slow that day.

He started to get worried when the officer did not clear him immediately. What was happening? Had they found out about the murder? He started fidgeting and became nervous. His heart was pounding and he contemplated making a run for it. But where could he go? He remembered seeing armed policemen in the airport. He started to regret his move and cursed himself for returning to Singapore. He did not have to wait long to realise that his worst nightmare had come true—two uniformed policemen were walking towards him. He knew they were there to arrest him.

The policemen told him he was wanted for questioning in connection with a crime, but did not say anything else. They seized the pouch he was carrying and handcuffed his wrists, then led him to the baggage claims section to retrieve his bags. He pointed to his black carrier bag and the green backpack on the conveyor. There was no point in pretending not to be able to identify the bags; they had numbered tags which were recorded in the flight register and the police would be able to trace them to him. After taking the bags, the officers led him to a room in the airport to wait for the arrival of the investigating officer.

In the room, he panicked and could not think straight. He broke out in cold sweat, fearing the consequences. He had read in newspapers and magazines back home that Singapore was not a country to be trifled with, and that its government was ruthlessly efficient. The justice system was tough on criminals too, and he had heard about the "notorious" Changi Prison.

He then became furious. He was mad at the police officers for arresting him and not telling him anything, and angry with himself for returning to Singapore. He shouted at the top of his voice and banged his head against the glass window; it broke with a loud noise and glass splinters fell to the floor. He picked up a piece with his right hand and used it to slash his left wrist. He felt a searing pain and the wound bled. An officer came in and ordered him to stop what he was doing. Eventually, he calmed down and sat quietly.

At about 10.40 pm, ASP Gerald Lim arrived. He had been with his girlfriend earlier, but had to cut short their date to go to the airport. His sidekick, Staff Sgt Zainal Abidin, had called to tell him that the airport police had arrested Davis, the suspect wanted in connection with the murder of South African tourist Lowe.

At the airport, he met the two officers who had arrested the suspect: Corporal Ang Keng Cheng and his partner, Norhisham Isnin. Cpl Ang briefed him on the arrest and commotion in the interrogation room. He also gave ASP Lim five passports recovered from the suspect.

ASP Lim looked at the passports. Two of them were British passports issued to the same man: Simon James Davis. There were two Canadian passports in the names of Sheila and Darin Damude, but the passports had the suspect's photographs stuck over the original photographs. The stamps on the passports indicated that the last destination was Bangkok. The last document was a South African passport. ASP Lim opened it and saw the name "Gerard George Lowe", but the photograph was that of the suspect. His instinct told him he had caught his man.

The South African passport was kept in a Miller

Weedon Travel holder. From the side compartments, ASP Lim found various cards belonging to Lowe, including his gold MasterCard, South African Breweries Medical Aid Society card, Mensa membership card, Avis and Imperial car rental cards, three business cards and a return South African Airways ticket to Johannesburg in the name of Lowe G.G. Also in the passport holder were the suspect's documents—a photocopy of Lowe's passport carrying the suspect's photograph, a lost-item report from the Tanglin Police Division in Singapore and a special Immigration pass issued by the British High Commission to Simon James Davis.

ASP Lim was certain that Lowe was dead as police had found torso, thighs and legs believed to be his. But he was bothered by the two Canadian passports found on the suspect. Who were these people and what had become of them? Had they been killed too?

At about 11.30 pm, ASP Lim examined the suspect's bags. One was a black carrier bag and the other, a green backpack. The black bag was secured with a tiny padlock. Both bags had name tags from Marco Polo Tours in Vancouver; the name "Davis Simon James" was on the tags.

About 20 minutes later, ASP Lim checked the black Eagle Creek brand canvas pouch that the suspect had hand-carried on the plane. He sat quietly at one side as the officer emptied its contents onto the table. Among the things in the pouch were US$1,600 worth of Royal Bank of Canada traveller's cheques, US$2,900 worth of American Express traveller's cheques, a Citibank chequebook, a Seiko calculator, photocopies of the Canadians' passports with the suspect's photographs on them and some receipts, including one issued by the Thomas Cook office in Singapore to Mr Simon Davis.

The officer was puzzled as there were also other documents bearing another name: a replacement British passport issued on November 28, 1994, by the British High Commission in Mexico City, an STA Travel Club Card, a Citibank card and a Mexican driving licence. All these were in the name of John Martin. The officer checked the photographs on both the passport and driving licence. The man in the photographs looked like the suspect in front of him. He looked up and stared hard: Who was this man? Was he Simon James Davis or John Martin?

ASP Lim asked the suspect for his name. The man replied, "I will not answer any questions until I see my lawyer or a representative from the British High Commission."

As he refused to cooperate, ASP Lim instructed Staff Sgt Michael Tan, a fellow CID officer, to take the suspect to the Alexandra Hospital for a medical examination, and to get the wound on his left wrist treated. He also ordered that the suspect's luggage be put in the same police vehicle conveying him to hospital. This was done so that the suspect would have no grounds to complain later that the police had slipped things into his bags while he was being taken to hospital.

It was already past midnight but ASP Lim knew he had a long day ahead. After the suspect was taken away, he told another officer, Sgt Kwok Nam, to collect and mark as evidence the bloodstains in the interview room. There was blood on the glass splinters, floor and chair.

At about 1.10 am, the suspect was taken to the Criminal Investigation Department. He was led into an interrogation room where his two bags were searched thoroughly. He still refused to answer any questions. From his pouch, the officers found a wallet containing various types of bank notes: S$1,700, US$186, Canadian $624, HK$350, NT$1,650, 165 Malaysian ringgit, 3,037 Thai baht, 390 Mexican pesos, 1,000 German marks, 110 Swiss francs, 140 Indian rupees, 60 South African rands and 38 units of Belize currency.

A second Eagle Creek brand black canvas pouch was also found on the suspect. From this pouch, the officers retrieved a gold Visa credit card belonging to a Jim W. Steiner, Sheila Damude's credit and bank cards, air tickets issued in the name of Sheila and Darin Damude and photocopies of the Canadians' passports. There were also some other documents, including a Singapore Post parcel posting receipt dated March 9 and a British birth certificate issued in the name of Simon James Davis.

After examining the pouches, the officers opened the small padlock securing the black carrier bag and took out its contents, item by item. There were a red hammer weighing 1.5 kg, a clipboard, some brown grassy substances, two Swiss Army knives, an oilstone for sharpening knives, a Police brand foldable knife, a diary, an organiser, a Gold Star computer chip, a set of handcuff keys, five packages of coins in various denominations,

Ray-Ban sunglasses, reading glasses inside a Ray-Ban case, two Aiwa speakers, Bushnell binoculars, an alarm clock, two unused Konica disposable cameras, a harmonica, five utensils wrapped in newspapers, two Sony Sports Walkmans, River View Hotel matches, skin care lotion, a Virgin brand eye mask, Oral B dental floss, a small beanbag, two bandannas, a felt pouch with pens, a bottle of Tiger Balm ointment, a book entitled *Thus Spake The Buddha*, several packs of condoms, a Coca-Cola towel and a few pieces of men's clothing including shirts, shorts and Lui, Cactus and St. Michael's briefs.

There was also an Eagle Creek toiletry pouch in the black carrier bag. It contained a facial wash, toothbrush, hairbrush, teaspoon, Paul Mitchell shampoo and conditioner, Axe deodorant, Nivea cream, Gillette shaving blades, Camay soap, several packets of condoms, ear plugs, cotton buds and Oxy 10 acne cream.

The officers then searched the green backpack which had belonged to Darin Damude. They found a battery-operated Z-Force III electrical stun device, a can of mace, two pairs of handcuffs, a pair of thumbcuffs, another Police brand knife and various men's and women's clothing. There were about 20 pieces of women's wear—including blouse, skirts, tights and floral shorts—tied together in a bundle with a red cotton belt.

There was also another toiletry bag in the green backpack. It contained more condoms, shampoo, foam bath and stirrer from the River View Hotel, a Walls ice-cream stick, a small bottle of rum, mosquito repellent and miscellaneous items.

From the suspect himself, the police seized a Citizen wristwatch, Cross pen, brown wallet and Singapore Airlines ticket in the name of Davis S.J. From the wallet, the police found US$546; a Singapore $2 note; 50 pesos worth of Mexican coins; a Royal Bank Visa credit card; bank, personal health care and international telephone calling cards belonging to Darin Damude; Darin's British Columbia driver's licence which had the suspect's photograph glued onto it; a $50 Singapore Telecom telephone card; and two business cards of the Thomas Cook office in Singapore.

Damning evidence was mounting by the minute but the suspect still refused to answer questions. Police had grounds to believe that he had killed Gerard George Lowe in Room 1511 of River View Hotel but there were insufficient details to draw up a specific murder charge. For example, when did the killing take place? It was already late evening on March 20 and the suspect had been in police custody for about 24 hours. Time was running out. Under Singapore law, the police could detain a person for not more than 48 hours without a court order. The suspect had to be produced before a judge by the following day at the latest.

At about 9 am on March 21, the tall Briton was led by police officers to the dock in Court 26 of Singapore's Subordinate Courts. He was handcuffed and sat beside a group of other men facing criminal charges that morning. There were more than 100 people present, including 10 journalists who knew that his case would be mentioned—that morning, *The Straits Times* had carried a report that a suspect had been arrested in connection with the body parts murder. A few minutes later, everyone stood up and remained quiet when they heard a loud bang on the floorboard, a signal that the district judge was entering the courtroom.

His case was among the first few to be heard. A court clerk read the charge aloud to him: "That you, Simon James Davis, 29, a British national, are charged with forging the signature of one Gerard George Lowe on a credit card transaction slip to obtain a S$6,000 cash advance on March 9."

The journalists were taken by surprise. Why a forgery charge? Wasn't the man in for a murder rap? Only the police knew the reason then. They needed more time to gather information and had settled for the subsidiary charge, one for which they had sufficient evidence (the bank's transaction slips and security video footage). Their purpose was to obtain a court order to detain him for another week.

The detectives swung into high gear even as the suspect was being charged in court. They picked up the leads that they had left off at the initial stage. One of the most fruitful steps was to follow up on the telephone calls made from Room 1511 between March 8 and 11. One of the calls was eventually traced to Danny Teo, the salesman who had tried to sell notebook computers to the suspect. He told the police he recalled seeing the suspect in his shop after 5 pm on March 8. He said the suspect had introduced himself as "Mr Lowe". Bingo.

Employees of River View Hotel were interviewed again. One of them, Tay Yue Mae, remembered that the suspect had approached her at about 8 am on March 9 to ask her to delete his roommate's name. The roommate was Gerard George Lowe. Bingo again.

The police also asked Scotland Yard in London for help in checking the background of Simon James Davis, and they wanted to know more about John Martin. They then made a startling discovery: Davis was not the man detained at the airport, but a different person altogether. The suspect had stolen Davis's birth certificate so that he could make a passport under that name. The suspect's real name was John Martin and he was 35 years old. Sometime in 1986, he had changed his name through deed poll; before that, he was known as John Martin Scripps. He was a jailed British drug trafficker who had absconded from prison in October 1994 during home leave.

At about 9 am on March 24, three days after his first court appearance, the suspect was taken to the Subordinate Courts again. This time, he was indicted with a fresh criminal charge: "That you, John Martin, 35, a British national, are charged with the murder of one Gerard George Lowe, in a River View Hotel room sometime between 12 noon on March 8 and 8 am on March 9." Under Singapore law, this charge carries a mandatory death sentence upon conviction.

After the charge was read out, District Judge S. Thyagarajan made an order for the accused to be placed in the Changi Prison hospital for psychiatric observation. This was to determine if he was mentally sound to face trial, should there be one. His next court mention was on April 17. Martin was then placed in a prison van and driven away from the Subordinate Courts complex in Havelock Road, a short distance from River View Hotel where he had killed his victim.

7

DEAD MEN TELL TALES

On March 24, while John Martin was being indicted in Singapore for the murder of the South African, something else was happening in Phuket, Thailand.

At about 11.50 am that day, the Thai police made another discovery of human body parts. This time, the body parts were found in some undergrowth along Bahn Nai Trang Road, about 900 m away from Nilly's Marina Inn. The parts were a skeletonised human torso and a pair each of decomposed arms and legs. The body parts were cut off at the joints. Police Major Anuruth Am-arb gave orders for them to be taken to the Vachira Hospital mortuary. Somehow, he knew that this find was related to the two skulls found at the disused tin mine in Kathu district, although the two locations were 9.7 km apart.

At the mortuary, Dr Roongrueng Kijphati, a forensic anthropologist, examined the skulls and human parts. One skull was smaller than the other. From its size, shape and dental features, it was determined that the smaller skull belonged to a female Caucasian. It still had a cervical bone attached to its base. The bone had been cut off neatly from the rest of the spinal cord and there was no damage to it. The skull had a sunken fracture measuring 8 cm by 4.5 cm on the top left portion. The depressed fracture was likely to have been caused by a single, heavy blow to the head. The impact resulted in a fracture line which went all the way from the top to the base of the skull. As the flesh had rotted away, Dr Kijphati could not conclusively determine the cause of death. He could only deduce that death was caused either by the fracture created by the single blunt force or the severance of the head from the neck.

The larger skull belonged to a male Caucasian. It had been severed at the second cervical bone and had a fracture, measuring 5 cm by 4.5 cm, on the right frontal side and nasal bone. As with the other skull, the fracture was caused by a single blunt force. The possible causes of death were also similar.

The arms were next. Both arms were in an advanced stage of decomposition. The flesh, which had turned a reddish-brown colour, was rotting and maggots were crawling about. The doctor found that each arm still had five fingers attached to the hands. The fingers were small and slender, indicating that the hands were those of a woman. The clean-cut edges of the flesh covering the humerus bones showed that the arms had been skilfully cut off from the shoulder joints with a sharp instrument, and there was no damage to the bones. It was possibly the work of a doctor or butcher. There was no open wound or other injury to the arms, and the doctor concluded that both arms belonged to the same woman.

The legs, which had been severed at the knees, were also badly decomposed. The flesh at the knee portions showed that the legs had been cut off from the thighs with a sharp instrument. There was no damage to the tibia bones and no injury or open wound on the legs. The shape of the feet showed that both legs probably belonged to the same woman.

The human torso was skeletonised. There were no internal organs but a bit of flesh remaining on the rib cage. The cervical spine had 28 discs attached to the sacrum. An adult normally has 29 discs in the spinal cord. All the cervical bones were intact. The right and the left sides of the ribs were also intact, and there were no fractures. Judging from the shape of the pelvic bone, the doctor was able to tell that the torso belonged to a woman.

Dr Kijphati attempted to fit the smaller skull onto the top part of the torso. It was a good fit. He concluded that there was a high possibility that the smaller skull and torso belonged to the same Caucasian woman. He believed that the four severed limbs also belonged to the same woman.

Apart from the skull, the rest of the male Caucasian's body parts remained missing.

The previous day, on March 23, Canadians Sheila and Darin Damude had officially been listed as missing. Singapore police had alerted the authorities in Thailand after the Damude's passports were found on Martin. Thai immigration records showed them entering the country via the airport in Bangkok, but there was no record of them leaving the country. There was no report of their passports being lost and they had not sought help from the Canadian Embassy.

The Royal Canadian Mounted Police had strong reason to believe they were murdered because their passports and personal items were found on the man whom the Singapore police had arrested for the murder of a South African tourist. The Canadian police believed that the body parts recovered in Phuket belonged to the missing mother and son. The killings were similar to the one in Singapore and the bodies of all the victims were dismembered.

The Canadian police had to confirm that the two skulls belonged to the Damudes. This would be done by comparing the dental features of the skulls with the Damudes' dental records. The Mounties' liaison officer in Bangkok, Brian H. Williams, was instructed to retrieve the pair's dental records from their hometown in Victoria, British Columbia. The records were handed over to the dental section of the Police General Hospital in Bangkok for forensic examination.

The dental comparison was done by Thai dentist Dr Surasak Choychumroon. He first examined the smaller skull. There were no fractures in the upper and lower jaws. The upper jaw had nine teeth while the lower, eight.

When comparing the features of the lower jaw with Sheila Damude's dental chart, Dr Choychumroon found five matches, including missing molars due to tooth extraction and amalgam fillings on certain teeth. But Sheila's chart had records of four other teeth which were not found on the skull's lower jaw. The doctor believed that the missing teeth had probably dropped out as a result of decomposition and there were open wounds on the sockets to support this theory.

As for the upper jaw, there were 12 matches with records on the chart. The Thai dentist was convinced that the smaller skull belonged to Sheila Damude. There were at least 17 similarities altogether. Also, going by the attrition and anatomy of the teeth, the estimated dental age was over 40 years. Sheila was 49.

The larger male skull had fractures in the upper and lower jaws. There were 14 teeth in the upper jaw and 14 in the lower jaw. Dr Choychumroon compared the skull's dental features with Darin Damude's dental records. The comparison of the upper and lower jaws with the chart was easier this time. The doctor found 19 perfect matches. There were only two differences. A molar on the lower jaw had a small cavity that was not reflected in the dental chart. The doctor believed that the cavity could have appeared after Darin last saw his dentist.

The other difference was that a pre-molar on the upper jaw had amalgam fillings on three surfaces, but the fillings were not shown in the chart. It was possible that Darin had gone to another dentist for this treatment. Dr Choychumroon was certain that he was examining Darin Damude's skull as there were so many similarities. Also, the dental age of the skull was estimated to be between 20 and 25 years. Darin was 23.

After it was confirmed that the Canadians had been murdered, Thai police began their inquiries. While a suspect had been arrested in Singapore for another crime, they still had to gather evidence of the killings in Phuket, in case the suspect was acquitted of the crime in Singapore. Until then, Thai police would not interfere with the Singapore police investigations.

On March 30, Major Am-arb arrived at Nilly's Marina Inn to conduct his probe. He seized two hotel registration cards. One showed that Sheila and Darin Damude had checked into Room 43 at about 5 pm on March 15. The other card showed that the suspect, who was using his assumed name of Simon James Davis, had checked into Room 48. But on March 16, the records showed that he had moved into the Canadians' Room 43, and the mother-and-son pair had not been seen since. The major also obtained the flight manifest of Thai Airways flight TG 213 from Bangkok to Phuket on March 15. On the passenger list were the names of Davis and the Damudes.

On April 2, Staff Sgt Zainal Abidin and Sgt Han Khoe Juan of the Singapore Police Force arrived in Phuket to work with Major Am-arb. They visited the disused mine and jungle, where the body parts had been found, to take photographs. They also went to the mortuary to photograph the human remains. The photographs would be tendered in court as evidence.

Next, the Singapore and Thai police officers went to Nilly's Marina Inn to interview its staff, especially Oy LoGate, who had served the suspect and Canadians. Later, in Room 43, they saw bloodstains on the wall, glass window, shower curtain and bed-skirt of one of the two beds.

The Scene of Crime officers from the Royal Thai Police were called in. They took swabs of the stains, removed the shower curtain and cut strips of cloth from the bed-skirt. These would be sent to the forensic laboratory for analysis.

The officers also looked for cabby Weerasak Wongpanich at the airport, and found him. Oy had informed them that he had driven the Canadians and the suspect to the hotel, and this was confirmed by the cabby. When he was shown a stack of photographs that Staff Sgt Zainal Abidin had brought with him from Singapore, he picked out Sheila Damude's floral bag. The woman was carrying this bag, he said.

Later, with the assistance of the Royal Canadian Mounted Police, photographs of the things found on John Martin were taken to British Columbia in Canada. They were shown to Sheila's sister, Karin Clarke, and good friend, Maja Briscoe, so that they could point out the items belonging to the Damudes.

The two women singled out 23 items which belonged to Sheila. These were a Woods backpack, Gucci wristwatch, Louis Vuitton wallet, Hotstuff hairdryer, fabric pouch, floral carrier bag, Oakley hardcover spectacles case, waist pouch, black and white patterned shorts, floral shorts, blue patterned pants, beige turtleneck pullover, light brown woman's jumpsuit, yellow jumpsuit, made-in-India jumpsuit, silk pyjamas, red woman's jumpsuit, floral woman's shorts, khaki bermudas, floral bermudas, white sleeveless blouse, three sleeveless tops and a floral shorts and blouse set. They also saw some Paul Mitchell products in the suspect's pouch and knew that Sheila used only this brand of toiletries.

As for Darin's belongings, they recognised his Bushnell binoculars, green backpack, pair of sunglasses and pieces of accessories strung into a necklace.

Meanwhile, Lowe's wife, Vanessa, had flown into Singapore from Johannesburg. Accompanied by ASP Gerald Lim, she went to the Criminal Investigation Department to assist the police in their probe into her husband's death. She was asked to look through more than 100 items seized from her husband's suspected killer. She saw things that were familiar to her, including the Institute of Breweries blue document bag which had a patch on the side. Her husband had accidentally brushed the bag against a hot machine and later patched the hole up with similar material from an old bag, she said. She also recognised the green-purple-black carrier bag that his sisters had given him for Christmas in 1993.

Other things familiar to her were her black leather waist pouch, a blue nylon toiletries bag, brown Woolworth's leather belt, pair of spectacles with a red neck sling, spectacle case with the words "Frames Unlimited", fake Rolex watch, integrated computer chip in a small Standard Bank plastic bag, Miller Weedon Travel passport holder, Lowe's South African passport, gold Standard Bank MasterCard, Imperial car rental card, Avis privilege card, Mensa South Africa card, Voyager silver card, South African Breweries Medical Aid Society card, business cards, South African Airways ticket, clipboard, Tuchenhagen calculator, Philips 1000 hairdryer and a tube of made-in-South Africa Colgate toothpaste. She could also recognise his maroon, blue and brown handkerchiefs; light blue, dark blue and red Woolworth's underwear with "G" markings on the labels; dark blue and dark red Edgar's underwear; beige Woolworth's bermudas; dusty blue Mauritius T-shirt; multi-coloured viscose short-sleeved shirt and green Woolworth's bermudas.

Vanessa also had to go through the agony of looking at the body parts. It had been a couple of weeks since they had been taken out of the sea. However, they had been washed, cleaned and preserved with chemicals. Still, it was difficult for her to look at them and she felt a surge of grief and anguish. Despite her tears, she recognised moles and freckles on the back of the torso, a 1-cm operation scar (for the removal of a cyst) on the rear right side, an appendectomy scar on the front right side, a bony lump below the knee of the right leg and the shape of the lower legs, feet and toes.

From these details, Vanessa knew that the police had found her husband.

8

PREPARATION FOR TRIAL

On April 6, ASP Gerald Lim and two other officers, Staff Sgt Michael Tan and Sgt Choy Ah Kiong, flew to London with an important package. It contained blood and forensic samples from the body parts murder in Singapore. While Vanessa had already identified the victim as her husband, the police needed an independent confirmation to make the case stronger in a court trial.

The package was prepared by Singapore's Department of Scientific Services. Among the samples were blood swabs taken from the bathroom of River View Hotel; swabs from the shower curtain; blood samples from Gerard's mother and sisters, Terry and Joanna; bone marrow samples extracted from the torso and a severed leg; blood sample from John Martin and a blood swab from his hammer, the murder weapon.

The Singapore officers were met on arrival by Detective Sergeants John Warren and David Cannon from Scotland Yard. Later, with the British officers' assistance, the package was handed over to the Wetherby Forensic Science Laboratory in West Yorkshire for DNA tests. The scientist conducting the tests was Michael John Barber.

Barber joined the Forensic Science Service in 1986 shortly after obtaining a Bachelor of Science degree (honours) in biochemistry. He had been working in the field of DNA analysis since 1988 and had testified in several hundred court cases. He was involved in the research, development and validation of the Short Tandem Repeat (STR) Profiling, an advanced technique used in forensic tests.

The test involves DNA amplification, targeting specific areas of the genetic material. This multiplies the areas many times, increasing the initial quantity of DNA and enabling results to be obtained even though the initial samples contained only minute traces of the genetic material being studied. This technique is widely used by forensic experts to compare materials such as blood, semen, saliva and hair root left at the scene of crime, to establish whether they could have originated from a particular person.

The amplification technique is applied to different areas of the DNA, such as the HUMVWA, HUMTHO1 and HUMPES. Each locus (DNA area) contains a structure called the STR. The STR loci vary in length from one person to another. With amplification, the STR loci are copied many times, enabling them to be seen as distinct bands. Each STR locus has two bands—one from each parent—but the inherited bands are sometimes similar in length and appear as one. This is known as the STR profile which can be used to determine a person's identity, through the process of comparison and deduction, because close relatives would have similarities in their profiles.

In the present case, Barber had to determine whether the body parts belonged to Lowe, if the blood in the River View Hotel bathroom was his and the source of the blood on Martin's hammer. Barber also conducted tests on the bloodstained cloth strips from Nilly's Marina Inn in Phuket, given to him by the Thai Police. This was his finding.

STR BANDS DETECTED IN THE SAMPLES

SAMPLE	HUMVWA	HUMTHO1	HUMPES	POSSIBLE SOURCE
BLOOD *(Mother's)*	19, 20	6, 7	11, 11	—
BLOOD *(Sister 1's)*	16, 19	7, 9.3	11, 11	—
BLOOD *(Sister 2's)*	16, 19	6, 9.3	11, 11	—
BONE MARROW *(Leg)*	16, 19	6, 7	11, 11	**Gerard Lowe**
BONE MARROW *(Torso)*	16, 19	6, 7	11, 11	**Gerard Lowe**
BATHROOM SWABS	16, 19	6, 7	11, 11	**Gerard Lowe**
SHOWER CURTAIN	16, 19	6, 7	11, 11	**Gerard Lowe**
BLOOD *(Martin's)*	14, 16	6, 6	5, 7	—
SWABS *(Hammer)*	15, 16	6, 9.3	—	**Unknown**
SWABS *(Phuket)*	15, 16	6, 9.3	—	**Unknown**

From the results of the tests, Barber found strong support for the assertion that the body parts belonged to Gerard George Lowe. This was because there were similarities in STR areas HUMVWA and HUMPES in samples taken from the body parts and those from his sisters. Only blood relations would produce such similarities. As for the bloodstains, Barber found extremely strong support for the assertion that the blood samples taken from the River View Hotel bathroom and those from the body parts had originated from the same person (Lowe) because all the STR areas were similar. For the Singapore police, the test erased all doubts that the South African had been murdered and his body dismembered.

The test also strengthened their suspicion that Martin had also murdered the Canadians because the blood found on his hammer was the same type as the blood found on the bed in the Phuket hotel. The source of the blood, however, could not be established—whether it was from the mother or son—as comparison samples were not available. But this was sufficient for the police. Reading this result in the light of other evidence found on Martin, such as the Canadians' passports and belongings, the police knew they had also found the Damudes' killer.

Meanwhile, the Singapore police officers in London sought help from Scotland Yard officers to conduct checks on the background of John Martin, known as John Martin Scripps to the British authorities. He had a long criminal record and had been in and out of jail for burglary, theft and drug trafficking. He was serving a 13-year jail sentence for trafficking heroin when he absconded in October 1994.

Between February 1992 and August 1993, he had been

in Her Majesty's Prison Albany on the Isle of Wight, England. On August 20, 1993, he was transferred to The Mount Prison in the north of London due to his being reclassified from a Category B to Category C prisoner. One of the main benefits for C prisoners, who were considered non-dangerous, was they could get home leave. It was during one of these home-leave periods that Martin escaped from Britain.

To leave the country, he used the birth certificate of fellow convict Simon James Davis to obtain a passport, and Davis became his assumed name while he was on the run. During this time, he visited several countries, including Mexico and the United States, before finding his way to Singapore and Thailand.

ASP Gerald Lim later met James Quigley, chief caterer at the Albany prison. Quigley knew Martin as John Scripps. He told ASP Lim revealing things about Martin, including the fact that he had mastered butchery skills. Forensic experts in Singapore and Thailand had said that the person who had cut up the bodies of Lowe and the Damudes was either a doctor, surgeon, veterinarian or butcher. Martin was a butcher.

Quigley said he first knew Martin when the latter worked in his kitchen as a dishwasher in February 1993. From there, he progressed to become a general cleaner and was put in charge of cleaning the kitchen and getting rid of waste. The prison caterer told ASP Lim, "Once I identified that he had potential for a more responsible job, he was offered the position of butcher. The prisoner accepted the challenge and received training from Ginger, another member of the catering staff and myself."

Martin was then taught butchery skills over a six-week period between March and April 1993. He was trained to bone out forequarters and hindquarters of beef, sides of bacon and carcasses of pork, and to portion chicken. The boning process required him to remove bones from the animal carcasses in such a way that the quality of the meat cuts was not impaired.

"This operation requires great skill with a knife. To obtain various cuts of meat would involve knowing where to cut at the joints and how to dissect the animal. He was also taught how to sharpen knives using a butcher's steel," said Quigley.

He said that Martin was a quick learner and was competent and confident in dissecting the different joints of meat from the carcass. After his initial training, he had total responsibility for preparing the various cuts of meat for the inmates' meals.

"He would report to my office every day to collect the knives necessary for carrying out his task. This became his department which he ran very efficiently on his own until he was transferred to The Mount Prison on August 20, 1993."

Back in Singapore, there was still work to be done. The police had to carry out an identification parade to see if witnesses could pick out John Martin as the man they saw. To do this, ASP Gerald Lim had to look for other Caucasian men to stand in the parade. In a country where the population was primarily Asian, where could he find these men? The police could not just ask anyone off the streets. Most Caucasians in Singapore were working expatriates and might not have the time or inclination to help. ASP Lim asked the embassies and got a few volunteers, but that was not enough.

His other option was to go to the budget hotels in Bencoolen Street, the haunt of many backpacking tourists. ASP Lim reckoned that, being the adventurous sort, they might be game to take part in a police line-up. It might be a cool thing to be able to tell the folks back home about what they did in Singapore. ASP Lim was right; he found the volunteers he needed.

The identification parade was carried out in a room with a one-way mirror. The suspect and volunteers stood in a brightly lit room facing the mirror. The witnesses would be led into the room behind the mirror, one by one, to see if they could pick out the suspect.

The time was 12.14 pm and the first witness was Danny Teo. He was asked to identify the man he had met on the evening of March 8 and again on March 9. He singled Martin out without hesitation. He also gave the police a note that he had written when he met the man. On it were the words, "Lowe, River View Hotel Room 1511".

The next witness was Armillah Johar. It was 12.24 pm and she was asked to point out the man she had served at Changi International Airport's hotel reservation counter on the morning of March 8. But she was unable to identify anyone.

At 12.36 pm, the witness was Chua Jee Noi, a Singapore Post clerk. She was asked to point out the man she had served at the post office in the Raffles City Shopping Centre on March 9. She was not able to identify anyone.

At 12.39 pm, River View Hotel cashier Julie Seah was asked to identify the man she had served at the check-out counter on March 11. She pointed at Martin.

It was 12.47 pm and the witness was another hotel employee, Cheah Chin Shyuan. She was asked to identify the man who had asked for the address of an Orchard Road coin shop on March 10. She pointed at Martin.

At 12.51 pm, the witness was the hotel's senior duty manager, Doreen Tan. She was asked to identify the man she had checked in together with Lowe. She pointed at Martin.

At 12.57 pm, the witness was Emily Tan Suan Kiow, the DBSBank teller in the Raffles City Shopping Centre. She was asked to identify the man who had made cash advances from Lowe's credit card on three occasions between March 9 and 10. She said she could not remember the man and was unable to identify anyone from the line-up.

At 1.05 pm, the witness was Tay Yue Mae, the hotel's banquet sales executive. She was asked to identify the man whom she had attended to on two occasions between March 9 and 10. She pointed at Martin.

At 1.12 pm, the witness was the hotel's security guard, Jamil Snane. He was asked to identify the man whom he had seen lugging a big, black suitcase out of the hotel early on March 11. He pointed at Martin.

At 1.18 pm, the witness was Thomas Cook employee Yvonne Lim. She was asked to identify the man whom she had served in her office in Anson Road on two occasions between March 9 and 10. She pointed at Martin.

At 1.25 pm, the witness was Thomas Cook Travel employee Koh Chew Li. She was asked to identify the man who had bought an air ticket from her on March 11. She pointed at Martin.

At 1.36 pm, the witness was electronics salesman Kelvin Lee. He was asked to identify the man who had bought a video recorder and a pair of speakers from his shop on March 9. He pointed at Martin.

At 1.41 pm, the witness was Thomas Cook employee Sara Eng. She was asked to identify the man who had gone to her office to transfer money to the United States on March 11. She pointed at Martin.

At 1.45 pm, the witness was another Thomas Cook employee, Eng Leng Siah. She was asked to identify the man whom she had seen leaving a carrier bag in the waiting area of her office on March 11. She pointed at Martin.

At 1.56 pm, the witness was Thomas Cook manager Ng Hsian Pin. He was asked to identify the man who had kicked up a fuss about his traveller's cheques in the Thomas Cook office on March 11. He pointed at Martin.

The identification parade was over at 2 pm. ASP Lim asked his officers to return Martin to the CID lock-up. He also thanked the volunteers for their help and gave them CID caps and pins as souvenirs. The backpackers were pleased; now they even had proof to show the folks back home when they talked about their time in the police station and how they had stood next to Martin, who had already made headlines in British newspapers as the "tourist from Hell".

ASP Lim later packed the passports and various documents seized from Martin and handed them to document examiner Ng Gek Kwee of the Department of Scientific Services. He also sent the Z-Force III electrical stun device to Professor Liew Ah Choy, head of the Electrical Engineering Department of the National University of Singapore, for examination.

On April 24, Martin appeared in the District Court where he was indicted with five more forgery charges and a vandalism charge. This brought the total number of forgery charges—for using Lowe's credit card fraudulently—to six. The vandalism charge was for breaking the glass window in the interview room at Changi International Airport. While Martin already faced a capital charge, it was the practice of the Singapore police to indict the suspect with other charges that would remain dormant pending the outcome of the murder trial. The police would proceed with the ancillary charges only if Martin was acquitted of murder. This was to ensure that he would not be able to walk out of jail until he had paid his dues for the other crimes.

About a week later, Martin was in court again to face five more charges. He was charged with the possession of dangerous or illegal weapons including the electrical stun device, the can of mace, two Police brand knives and a hammer. He was also charged with the possession of controlled items (two pairs of handcuffs and a pair of thumbcuffs) and controlled drugs (24 sticks of cannabis). With these charges, Martin faced a total of 12 ancillary charges, apart from the murder charge which carried a mandatory death penalty.

Under Singapore law, a person convicted of carrying offensive weapons without a lawful purpose can be jailed for up to three years and receive at least six strokes of the cane. For the possession of controlled drugs, the penalty is a maximum 10 years' jail and a $20,000 fine. The maximum punishment for the illegal possession of handcuffs is one month's jail and a $1,000 fine. Vandalism is punishable with a maximum of three years' jail and eight strokes of the cane. Forgery is punishable with up to seven years' jail. Even if Martin, by sheer good fortune, managed to escape the death penalty, he would still be in a lot of trouble.

On September 18, a preliminary inquiry was held to determine if the prosecution had sufficient evidence to commit Martin to stand trial in the High Court for the murder of Lowe in the River View Hotel. He would not be tried for the murder of Canadians Sheila and Darin Damude because their deaths occurred in Phuket, outside the jurisdiction of the Singapore court. Conducting the trial for the prosecution was Deputy Public Prosecutor Jennifer Marie. The DPP was no newcomer to murder trials and had secured convictions in other cases. She was assisted by two junior DPPs, Toh Han Li and Norul Huda Rashid.

During the inquiry, DPP Marie produced the names of 77 witnesses. The list was eventually shortened to about 20 because most of the witnesses were police officers who were only involved in procedural and undisputed matters, such as the taking of photographs and the recovery of the body parts from the sea. Some of the main witnesses who would testify in court included Gerard's widow, Vanessa Lowe, British DNA expert Michael Barber, British prison caterer James Quigley, Thai anthropologist Dr Roongrueng Kijphati and Singapore senior forensic pathologist Prof. Chao Tzee Cheng.

After hearing a summary of the prosecution's case, Magistrate Karolyn Gin held that there was sufficient evidence to commit Martin to stand trial for the murder of Lowe. She fixed October 2, 1995, as the commencement date of the hearing in the High Court.

9

MY BRITISH FRIEND AND I

John Martin suffered the ignominy of scoring a string of firsts in the annals of Singapore crime. He was the first Briton to be charged with the capital offence of murder. If convicted, he would also be the first Briton to be executed by hanging in Singapore. He was the first criminal to be tried in the Singapore High Court's Technology Court, equipped with computers for the judge and counsel, a giant TV screen and various electronic features. For the first time, gruesome pictures of a murderer's deed—the severed body parts—were flashed on the screen for all in the courtroom to see.

Martin was the first British serial killer caught and tried in Singapore. While he was only charged with the murder of South African Gerard George Lowe in Singapore, the prosecution intended to lead evidence to show that he had also killed Canadians Sheila and Darin Damude in Phuket, Thailand.

Singapore has long abolished the jury system and a judge sits in all court cases, whether civil or criminal. The accused is entitled to select his own counsel and if he does not or cannot, the State assigns one to him. In capital cases, two lawyers are assigned to ensure that the accused gets the best possible defence he is entitled to under the law.

The lawyers assigned by the State to Martin were Edmond Pereira and Joseph Theseira, two experienced criminal lawyers. The judge who would decide the accused's fate was Justice T.S. Sinnathuray, a senior member of Singapore's Supreme Court Bench who was experienced in the area of criminal law.

On October 2, the first day of the trial, the courtroom was packed with about 20 journalists, half of them from Britain. They had flown to Singapore to cover the sensational story about their countryman who had gone globetrotting for victims. Also in the courtroom was Douglas Herda, the Royal Canadian Mounted Police liaison officer in Singapore who kept a watching brief over affairs concerning the Canadians.

At about 9.50 am, 10 minutes before court commenced, Martin was led into the room handcuffed and escorted by five prison officers. He smiled at journalists as he was being herded into a cubicle at the back. He also nodded to his lawyers, who had donned their black robes in readiness for the trial. He avoided eye contact with prosecutors Jennifer Marie, Toh Han Li and Norul Huda Rashid, who sat beside his lawyers.

Inside the cubicle, which had a big glass panel, Martin's handcuffs were removed but his legs were shackled to the iron bars beneath his seat. The authorities were not taking any chances; if what they knew about him was true, he was indeed a cunning and cold-blooded killer. Outside the courtroom were more armed guards wearing bullet-proof vests: the elite prison officers trained in assault and emergency procedures. Their role was to ensure that no one could disrupt the proceedings or take Martin away from being dealt with by the law.

Martin himself acted confidently, chatting casually with his guards as he waited for the trial to begin. He had already worked out his defence to the charge and was certain he would be able to escape the death sentence. He would surprise the prosecution. He knew it was difficult for him to deny that he had killed Lowe—after all, too many of the victim's possessions had been found on him. It would be foolish to deny the fact as it would make him appear even more guilty.

Rather, he would "come clean". He would confess that he had killed, but it was an accident; the other man had attacked him first and he was only defending himself. He knew this would earn him a long time in prison for culpable homicide not amounting to murder but at least it was not death. He was used to prison life.

So on April 4, months before the trial, he had asked ASP Gerald Lim to see him in prison. He gave the police officer a statement which formed the crux of his defence. It read:

On March 8, 1995, early in the morning, I arrived in Singapore from San Francisco, USA, on board a United Airlines flight. On arrival, I found the hotel reservation counter closed. I then tried calling a few hotels from the Yellow Pages but most were fully booked; those that were not were too expensive. I therefore remained at the Singapore Changi Airport until the hotel reservation counter opened later in the morning. I had come to Singapore on my way to Thailand to buy men's high-fashion clothes for the clothing shop that I plan to open in Mexico.

When the hotel reservation counter opened for business, I approached the staff to book a hotel room. I specified my budget, which was below US$100. I was the first person at the counter. There was another male Caucasian standing behind me, waiting to be attended to. While the staff was phoning various hotels to see whether they had a room, I chatted with the male Caucasian. He introduced himself as Lowe something and I introduced myself as Simon Davis. I cannot recall his other names but it begins with the letter "G". Before this, I did not know who Mr Lowe was. He told me he was in Singapore to buy electronic goods for his home in South Africa.

Most of our conversation was just small talk and I cannot recall it now. By this time, Mr Lowe was also going through a list of hotels. I cannot remember who suggested sharing rooms but I believe it was the reservation staff. She told us there was a vacant twin-bedded hotel room at the River View Hotel. Since it was difficult to get a hotel room, Mr Lowe and I agreed to share the room. We then left the airport together in a taxi and proceeded to the River View Hotel. I cannot recall who paid for the taxi fare.

On arriving at the hotel, we were told that the hotel

room was not ready and we were not able to check in yet. We then left our luggage at the hotel. I only had a black backpack and a small cotton bag. As for Mr Lowe, he had a suitcase and a carrier bag.

I saw Mr Lowe making some enquiries and the next thing I knew, both of us were in a taxi proceeding to Orchard Road. I cannot remember who paid for the taxi fare but I do remember that we took turns to pay for the taxi fares. By this time, I was already very tired. Nevertheless, I followed Mr Lowe through some electronic shops in Orchard Road. We also had some coffee together, mostly for keeping myself awake.

Sometime later, we returned to the River View Hotel by taxi. Mr Lowe did not purchase anything. At the hotel, we were told that our room was ready. We therefore checked ourselves in. The reception staff asked for our passports and I handed her a British passport under the name of Simon James Davis. I cannot remember the passport number. I had used the said passport to prevent getting detected as I am wanted in the United Kingdom for absconding from prison during my home leave. We then proceeded to our hotel room which was either on the 11th or 15th floor. The room number was either 1115 or 1511.

In the hotel room, I saw two twin-sized beds. I decided to have the bed away from the windows, next to the toilet. Mr Lowe told me to take a shower first as I appeared to be very tired. I agreed. I then unzipped my black backpack which was on a wooden bench. All my stuff fell out. I then took hold of my Cola-Cola towel and black toiletries bag from the stuff without packing it nicely back into my black backpack.

After taking my shower in the toilet, I came out and laid on the bed that I had chosen. I was wearing a pair of short pants and was naked from my waist up. After taking my shower, I towelled myself dry with a towel from the hotel. I did not use my own Coca-Cola towel and hung it in the toilet. After I came out from the toilet, Mr Lowe went in. I subsequently fell asleep.

I do not know for how long I had slept, but I was subsequently awakened when I felt a hand touching me on my buttocks. When I looked up, I saw Mr Lowe standing over me, smiling at me. He was wearing only a pair of underwear. I am not a homosexual and at that time, it appeared to me that Mr Lowe was a homosexual. I freaked out and quickly kicked out at him. At the same time, I shouted obscenities at him and asked him to keep away from me. I do not know where exactly on his body I had kicked but the impact caused him to keel backwards onto the dressing table. By this time, he was also shouting at me although I could not make out what he was saying.

Mr Lowe began throwing things at me. He flung my black toiletries bag which was placed on the dressing table, bits of clothes and the hammer that I use for camping and that was kept in my black backpack together with other camping equipment at me. My black toiletries bag hit me in the face while the hammer hit me in the stomach. He then came towards me and I used the hammer, which was held in my right hand, to hit him several times on the head until he collapsed onto the carpeted floor.

When I realised what I had done, I threw the hammer

onto Mr Lowe's bed. I then noticed that my right hand was covered with blood. Mr Lowe remained motionless on the floor. He was bleeding profusely from the head. However, I did not notice whether the carpet was stained with his blood. Mr Lowe had collapsed with his head facing the direction of the toilet and his body was on its side. However, I cannot remember whether it was the right or left side.

Everything happened so quickly. I then dragged Mr Lowe's body to the toilet. I slumped Mr Lowe's body over the bathtub with his head in the tub. I switched on the water tap and used running water to wash off the blood from his head. At the same time, I slapped Mr Lowe on his face and also shook him but he did not respond. I could see that Mr Lowe was not breathing because his chest was not moving up and down. I then panicked.

By this time, I also had blood on my left hand. I quickly washed the blood off my hands and slipped into a pair of jeans, a shirt and a pair of sandals. I do not recall having blood on my body. I then left the hotel room. When I reached the hotel lobby, I saw that it was still daylight. I did not notice the time although I do own a Citizen wristwatch. At the time, I was not wearing my wristwatch.

I then left the River View Hotel to find a British male friend at another hotel, someone I was supposed to meet in Singapore. I cannot tell you who this British friend is or which hotel he stayed in. I do not know how long he had been staying in Singapore prior to my arrival. I had phoned him from the USA when he was in the UK sometime in February 1995, and he had told me that he would be staying at this particular hotel in Singapore. I normally keep in touch with him once a month. I had tried calling him up at the hotel he was staying in when I first arrived in Singapore but he was not in his room the whole time. This was done from Changi Airport.

That day (March 8), I arrived at my friend's hotel in a taxi. I asked the hotel reception for his room number and they told me. I then proceeded to his room. After answering my knock on the door, my friend opened the door and let me in. I told him what had happened. He then told me to stay in his room and not to leave or open the door to anyone. He took the key to my room at the River View Hotel, which is in the form of a plastic card, and left.

Sometime later on the same day in the night, my friend returned and told me there was nothing to worry about as he had already got rid of Mr Lowe's body. He told me he had got rid of the body by throwing it into a river. However, he did not tell me how he managed to do this or which river he had thrown Mr Lowe's body into. He told me that I could now return to my hotel room at the River View Hotel. I did not want to but he told me that I must, so as not to create suspicion. Nevertheless, I remained with him that night in his hotel room and only returned to my room at the River View Hotel early the next morning. That night, I never left my friend's hotel room at all.

While staying at my friend's hotel room that night, he handed me Mr Lowe's South African passport which was kept in a white passport holder. My friend also pointed out to me that Mr Lowe's gold MasterCard and other documents were inside the passport holder. He told me to replace Mr Lowe's passport photograph with my photograph, which I did. I got a copy of my passport-size photograph from a little green plastic holder which contained several copies of my passport-size photographs which I normally keep in one of my two black clutch pouches. I believe my friend had also gone through my things and was able to find my passport-size photographs.

I used a stick glue provided by my friend to glue one of my passport-size photographs onto Mr Lowe's passport after I had carefully torn Mr Lowe's passport photograph from the passport. Below the photograph was Mr Lowe's signature which I removed and replaced by gluing on a similar yellow coloured piece of paper and signed "G. Lowe" on it. I did all this in my friend's hotel room. I cannot recall where I had obtained the yellow piece of paper. The signature that I forged was nothing similar to that of Mr Lowe's signature. I did not practise signing Mr Lowe's signature at the time.

My British friend then told me to use Mr Lowe's passport and gold MasterCard to draw out S$12,000 from a bank in the form of a cash advance, which I later did the following day from a bank at Raffles City. However, the bank only gave me S$6,000. My friend wanted this money for having assisted me in getting rid of Mr Lowe's body. He also told me that I owed him a favour.

I left my British friend's hotel sometime on the morning of March 9 and returned to the River View Hotel. Back at the hotel, I went to the hotel reception counter to extend my stay at the hotel. I paid my hotel bills in cash. On returning to my hotel room, I found everything neat and tidy. All my things were neatly put away in my black backpack and it was properly tied up. Besides my backpack, I also noticed Mr Lowe's suitcase. I noticed that all my belongings were kept back into my backpack. I did not see any of Mr Lowe's belongings except for his suitcase. I did not see what was inside the suitcase. I also do not know whether there was anything inside the suitcase. I also cannot remember what happened to the suitcase.

When I checked out of the hotel on March 11, the suitcase was no longer in the hotel room. It may be possible that my British friend had returned to get rid of the suitcase as he still had the key to the hotel room. There were two keys to the room; one was issued to me while the other was issued to Mr Lowe. The beds were all nicely made up. On looking into the toilet, Mr Lowe's body was no longer there.

I searched for my black pouch containing my Thomas Cook and American Express traveller's cheques, cash and my passport in the name of Simon James Davis but could not find it. I had about US$7,000 to US$8,000 worth of Thomas Cook traveller's cheques which I purchased in the USA and about £5,000 worth of American Express traveller's cheques which I purchased from Mexico. I had about £3,000 in cash and a collection of foreign currencies.

I am not sure what was the next thing I did but I do remember reporting it missing to the police. I then went down to the British Embassy [sic] *to get a replacement passport in the name of Simon James Davis. I also went to the Thomas Cook office in Singapore to cancel my Thomas Cook traveller's cheques. As a matter of fact, everything was such a blur to me after this incident that I was walking around in a dream world for the next few days.*

As for my British friend, I met him daily at either his hotel room or in Orchard Road. He was not satisfied with the S$6,000 that I had given him after drawing it using Mr Lowe's credit card from the bank at Raffles City and demanded for more. I then drew out more money a few more times using Mr Lowe's credit card but cannot recall the amounts. I handed all this money to my British friend as he wanted it for having gotten rid of Mr Lowe's body. I also did not want the money as it was "blood" money.

Since I was at the Raffles City Shopping Centre, I went looking for a birthday present for my elder sister, Janet Scripps. I subsequently decided to purchase her a video recorder. I had meant to use cash to pay for the video recorder but since I had Mr Lowe's credit card, I decided I might as well use it to purchase the video recorder. After purchasing the video recorder, I mailed it to my sister in the United Kingdom from the post office at Raffles City.

The day I was about to leave Singapore for Thailand, my British friend handed back to me my black pouch containing my Simon James Davis passport as well as all my traveller's cheques. He, however, kept all the cash. I begged him to return me my cash but he refused. I then left it as that. By that time, I had also received my replacement British passport in the name of Simon James Davis from the British Embassy [sic]. *I bought my air tickets to Thailand from Thomas Cook in Singapore. I also sent some money back to my bank account in the USA through Thomas Cook in Singapore. As I had no cash left with me, I cashed in my traveller's cheques to send the money back.*

The next thing I knew, I was in Bangkok, Thailand. I do not know which hotel I stayed in while in Bangkok. But when I was there, I realised that I had no more traveller's cheques. However, I had some cash left over from the exchange I had done at Thomas Cook in Singapore. On the same day that I arrived in Bangkok, I met up with my British friend. I cannot tell you the hotel he was staying in. We did not fly in together. I do not know whether he arrived in Bangkok first or I did. But I knew where to contact him as he had told me the hotel that he would be staying in Bangkok. We were not living together at the same hotel. In my friend's hotel room, I saw my collection of foreign currencies in a plastic pouch which I had kept the money in. I quickly took the foreign currencies back. I do not remember whether my friend had objected. I also later found, back at my hotel room, some clothes and a Rolex wristwatch, which I believed belonged to Mr Lowe, in my black backpack.

In the statement, John Martin also answered some of ASP Gerald Lim's questions.

Q: What do you know about the two Canadians whose passports were found in your possession?

A: As far as I remember, I have never met the two Canadians. It was my British friend who handed to me a plastic bag containing their Canadian passports, credit cards, some traveller's cheques and documents at the airport in Phuket, prior to my return to Singapore.

Q: On the day of the incident, on March 8, did you go straight to your British friend's hotel after the incident?

A: Yes, I did. I walked for a short distance looking for a taxi and subsequently found one and proceeded to my friend's hotel.

Q: When did you leave your British's friend's hotel after having arrived there on March 8?

A: I did not leave my friend's hotel until the following morning, March 9. I had remained at his hotel room throughout the night on March 8.

Q: When did you get your two pairs of handcuffs, thumbcuffs, electrical stun device and can of mace and what are they used for?

A: I bought the can of mace and electrical stun device in America and they are used to chase away stray animals. I cannot recall where the handcuffs and thumbcuffs came from as they do not belong to me.

Q: Did your British friend tell you what he did to Mr Lowe's body?

A: He did not specifically tell me what he did to the body but he did tell me that he had thrown the body into a river, or words to that effect.

Q: Do you know where this British friend is now?

A: No, I do not.

Q: Who is this British friend of yours?

A: I cannot tell you his identity because if he knew, he would harm my family back in the United Kingdom.

Q: How did you first meet him?

A: I first met him many years ago through his brother.

Q: Where did you get the two Police brand knives from and what are they used for?

A: One of it belongs to me while the other, I believe, belongs to my British friend. I do not know how this knife came into my possession. It is actually a camping knife. Almost everyone in England carries one. England was where I got it from. I also carry a Swiss pocket knife.

Q: You only had a black backpack. However, when you were arrested, you also had a green backpack. How did you come into possession of this green backpack?

A: My British friend gave it to me when I was in Bangkok.

Q: Did you go to Phuket, Thailand?

A: Yes, I did.

Q: Did you go there alone?

A: No, I went there with my British friend.

Q: Why did you return to Singapore from Thailand on March 11?

A: I was so confused as to what had happened to Mr Lowe. As such, I subconsciously returned to Singapore.

Q: Did your British friend return to Singapore with you?

A: No, he did not return to Singapore with me.

From his statement, it was obvious that Martin intended to push the bulk of the blame on this mysterious British friend of his. He might have killed the South African accidentally but no, he was not the one who had cut him up. Although he did not say so directly, he was implying to the police that the friend had dismembered the body. After all, the friend was supposedly the one who had dumped the body into the river. By not appearing to be the vicious man who had cut up the body of another, his story about the sexual attack in the hotel room would sound more convincing.

He flatly denied having anything to do with the Canadians' death as he could not provide any excuse for killing them. One accidental death might be believable but a second and third? He could not say that he was fending off another sexual attack. Coming from a mother and son, that would be ridiculous. The best way out of this mess was to deny everything. And in not so many words, he also implied to the police that his British friend had killed the Canadians, since the man gave him all their belongings. How convenient. If the police asked questions about his friend, he would say that this man, who was a drug lord, would wipe out his entire family if he squealed on him.

The prosecution was not to be confused by Martin's incredulous tale. The DPPs spotted many loopholes and saw through many layers of lies—they intended to shoot down every one with hard evidence. They would show that the so-called "British friend" did not exist and was created by Martin to save himself. They intended to use his own statement to counter his lies.

If it could be proven that the friend did not exist, the story about how the friend threw the body parts into the river would then be Martin's inherent confession to his own crime. This was because only the killer himself would know how the body was disposed of.

10

GOING FOR THE KILLER

Deputy Public Prosecutor Jennifer Marie had lined up about 20 prosecution witnesses for her case. Initially, there were more but in view of the path that John Martin had chosen, many were no longer necessary. For example, the fact that the body parts belonged to Gerard George Lowe was not challenged by the defence. Thus, witnesses were not required to support this fact. The issue before the court was not whether Martin had killed Lowe, but whether he did it intentionally or accidentally, as claimed.

The first witness was Lowe's widow, Vanessa. She was asked to fly to Singapore from Johannesburg to refute Martin's claim that her husband was a homosexual who had tried to have sex with him. Vanessa had prepared herself for the trial. Her husband's death had already caused her severe trauma and now, his killer was out to tarnish his name by calling him a homosexual. She was not going to let him get away with it and had sworn to defend her husband's reputation. She was determined to keep her composure in the witness box as crying would not do any good if she failed to counter the allegations.

And she succeeded. On the witness stand, she answered all questions calmly.

She first confirmed an earlier statement she had given to the police. In it, she said that she and her husband had been happily married and had a normal sexual relationship, and he was definitely not a homosexual. She said the sole purpose of his coming to Singapore was to shop. For this, he had brought along an empty black suitcase with red straps in which to carry his purchases. He also had black plastic bags to wrap the things up.

The DPP asked if her husband was the type who liked to walk about in the house in his underwear. Vanessa said, "No." What about in the company of other men, the DPP asked. "Definitely not. He would not walk around in underwear in the company of strangers."

It was the defence's turn to question her. Counsel referred to her statement to police which stated, "He was definitely not a homosexual and had despised homosexuals. He had told me that should he have a son who turned out to be a homosexual, he would disown him."

Counsel: Why did he say that?
Vanessa: He seemed to be very anti-homosexual.
Counsel: Do you personally despise homosexuals?
Vanessa: No.
Counsel: When he said that to you, what was your reaction?
Vanessa: I said to him that there were all types of people in this world. You just have to accept them for what they are.

Counsel: Do you know whether your husband had friends who were homosexuals?
Vanessa: No. Not as far as I know.

The next witness was Prof. Chao Tzee Cheng. The senior forensic pathologist was called to testify because he had performed autopsies on the body parts which were recovered from the sea off Clifford Pier. He noted that all the parts had been skilfully disarticulated at the joints. To show what he meant by cutting at the joints, the affable professor demonstrated to the court by using human bone specimens that he had brought along from his laboratory. He did this amid chuckles from the press gallery.

On a more serious note, he referred to autopsy pictures of the body parts which were flashed on the giant monitor. He said that the parts had clean-cut edges, indicating that they had been cut with a sharp-edged instrument. This instrument was not likely to be a big one as the parts had been cut off with several strokes. They were then separated skilfully as there were no injuries or fractures to the bones. Prof. Chao said that the man who did this must be knowledgeable about joints as he had to cut through the tendons before disarticulating. He said, "This person has to be a veterinarian, doctor, surgeon or butcher. When I saw the parts, I immediately told police we could be dealing with a serial killer."

Prof. Chao said the body could have been dismembered within half an hour as the procedure did not require a lot of physical strength. He added that if the body parts were drained of all blood, the packing could be done within an hour. That meant that cutting and packing would only take about one-and-a-half hours. When shown Martin's two Police brand knives with serrated blades, the professor said they could be used to cut body parts from the joints. He pointed out that the blades could produce clean, straight cuts as they facilitated the sawing motion.

He said the body was dismembered after the victim had died. However, he could not determine the cause of death as the head had not been found. There were bruises on the back on the torso and around the neck, but none of the impact injuries could have caused death. He also had one finding which supported Vanessa's testimony that her husband was not a homosexual: "The anus was not dilated and there was no injury. What I meant was that it was in its pristine and original condition, not tampered with by anal sex."

On whether the parts would generate a foul smell if kept in the hotel room, Prof. Chao said that the decomposing parts would produce a very strong smell if they were exposed. But the smell might be contained if they were wrapped and kept inside a suitcase. The process of decomposition could also be slowed down if the temperature of the room was lowered by air-conditioning. He said, "The smell of death is like the smell of salted fish. You must know it to detect it." The smell also lingers in the air and adheres to objects or persons close to it. "That is why we always need to take showers after performing autopsies. Otherwise, people will be running away from us," Prof. Chao said, causing others in the courtroom to laugh.

But one couple did not run away from the smell of death. The Indonesian couple who checked into River View Hotel Room 1511 after Martin left had detected a persistent foul smell but did not report it. The couple only found out that a grisly murder had taken place prior to their arrival when Staff Sgt Zainal Abidin flew to Indonesia to look for them.

Businesswoman Fransiska Wijaya Heuw told the officer that she and her fiance had checked into the room at about 10 pm on March 11. "When we entered the room, I noticed a foul smell. The smell was strong and I could not figure out what caused it. It appeared that the smell could have come from the carpeted floor near the bed." She also noticed that the bathtub and sink had yellowish stains on them but she did not see any blood. The couple occupied the room from March 11 to March 14 despite the smell.

The next witness was James Quigley, chief caterer of Her Majesty's Prison Albany. He said Martin had the skills to dismember a human body. He said that he and Ginger, a professional butcher, had trained Martin personally. From March to April 1993, Martin was trained to bone out forequarters and hindquarters of beef, sides of bacon, and the carcasses of pork and chicken without impairing the quality of the meat. Quigley said that Martin was competent and a quick learner and was left in charge of the butchery department which he ran very efficiently on his own until he was transferred to another prison in August 1993.

The prosecutor then produced Martin's two Police

brand foldable knives and showed them to the witness. He examined each knife and said, "This is the perfect instrument for deboning." He said both knives had sharp points which made it easier to make the first incision. A boning knife usually has a short blade with a very sharp point so that it can get between the bones and cut away the parts.

The experienced butcher also pointed out that the anatomy of a human and an animal, such as a cow or pig, was basically the same. "Humans have two main joints, the hinge joints at the knee and elbow, and a ball and socket joint at the hip and shoulder." He said that if he were to cut off a human arm, he would cut around the flesh to ascertain where the joint was. Once the tendons and ligaments were cut through, the next step would be to twist the arm out of the socket. This was what a butcher would do when he cut animals. When Quigley was asked how long he would take to cut one joint, he said without hesitation, "Five minutes."

While Quigley had been a butcher for more than 20 years, it was probably the first time he had been asked to describe how a butcher would cut up a human—and in an open court too. His confidence remained unshaken throughout but he did not appear to be amused when the defence counsel accidentally referred to the knives in his kitchen as "weapons".

After showing that Martin had the skills and equipment to kill, the prosecution introduced the next group of witnesses who would testify that the killing was premeditated, and that Martin had hatched the plan to kill and rob Lowe. The hotel reservation clerk at Changi International Airport, Armillah Johar, was called to testify. She said she remembered that Martin and Lowe had approached her counter together at about 8 am on March 8. "They appeared to have known each other because they were talking as if they were friends." She added that Martin made most of the enquiries and asked for a room with twin beds. She disputed the defence's suggestion that Martin came to her alone and that Lowe, who was waiting behind in the queue, somehow got into the picture and agreed to share a room when it was made known that single rooms were not available.

Another witness, Danny Teo, testified that Martin had gone to his electronics shop sometime after 5 pm on March 8. Martin told him he was planning to buy four notebook computers that he hoped to sell in Mexico for a profit, to cover his airfare to Singapore. The purchases would be paid for by credit card (Martin himself did not have any credit card). Danny said that the following day, he called Martin up and subsequently visited him in his hotel room to persuade him to buy the computers. He said he called Martin "Mr Lowe" at all times and the latter did not correct him. He remained in the room for about an hour but did not suspect that anything was amiss. He did not notice anything unusual as he was only interested in selling his computers.

Danny's testimony that Martin came to his shop on the evening of March 8 was unfavourable to the defence and contradicted Martin's claim that during that time, he was at his British friend's hotel room. The defence challenged Danny's account.

Counsel: I put it to you that you have made a mistake with the time, and that you saw the accused at your shop in the late morning of March 8, and not after 5 pm.

Danny: No. It was in the evening. I can definitely remember as he was the only customer who had come in to buy that many notebook computers on that day.

The next witness was River View Hotel banquet sales executive, Tay Yue Mae. She testified that while she was on duty at about 8 am on March 9, Martin came and asked her whether Lowe had collected his room deposit. He told her he had discovered the previous night that Lowe was gay. He had returned Lowe's share of the $250 deposit and "sent him packing". She said she then checked the computer and noted that Lowe had not checked out at all.

Martin then asked her to remove Lowe's name from the guest register leaving his name, "Simon James Davis". He informed her that he might stay another night and would return to pay the deposit after lodging a police report on his missing passport. Tay noted that Martin spoke in a gentle manner throughout and was not aggressive or agitated. "He appeared normal," she said.

The next witness was a crucial one for the prosecution as he was the only one who had seen Martin apparently trying to get rid of the body parts. The testimony of hotel security guard Jamil Snane would counter Martin's version that his British friend had helped to throw the body away. Speaking with the help of an interpreter, the Malay guard testified that he was on duty at the hotel lobby at about 6.30 am on March 11 when he saw Martin walking past him towards the hotel entrance. He said Martin was carrying a big, black suitcase with red straps and that the load appeared to be heavy.

The tall, slightly hunched man, who was wearing a "green, flowery Hawaiian short-sleeved shirt" and trousers, started to drag the suitcase when he reached the porch and headed left (the Singapore River is behind the hotel). Jamil said the man returned 15 minutes later without the suitcase, wiped his feet on the carpet, dusted his hands and walked towards the lift.

The defence launched an attack against the guard's testimony, saying that he had only caught a fleeting glance at the man supposedly carrying a suitcase that morning, and had mistaken him for Martin. The defence argued that Jamil identified Martin as the man because he had seen the accused's photograph, shown to him by police officers and published in the newspapers. Also, Martin did not have a "green, flowery Hawaiian shirt", but a green shirt with cowboy and Indian motifs.

Counsel: I put it to you that the male Caucasian you saw was not the accused?

Jamil: No. It was him.

Counsel: I put it to you that you said it was him because you had seen his photograph published in the newspapers.

Jamil: I am illiterate. I don't read newspapers.

Counsel: I put it to you that the reason why you identified the accused as the person you saw was because you were also shown his photograph by the police.
Jamil: I would have recognised him anyway, even without the photograph.

The turning point came when the prosecution intended to adduce "similar fact evidence" relating to the Canadians' death in Thailand to show that Martin was a cold-blooded murderer. The defence objected to this and argued that the controversial Thai evidence was irrelevant because the defendant was not on trial in Singapore for the murder of Sheila and Darin Damude. To accept the evidence would mean that the Singapore court would also have to rule that Martin was guilty of those murders. This, the defence argued, was outside the jurisdiction of the court as the Canadians' deaths took place outside Singapore. The Thai evidence should, therefore, be viewed as prejudicial and would interfere with the real evidence in the present charge.

The prosecution, in rebutting the argument, submitted that its purpose in admitting in the Thai evidence was not to show that the accused had the propensity to commit murder simply because he was linked to the killing of the Canadians. Rather, it was to rebut Martin's defence that the killing of Lowe was the result of "an unfortunate one-off buttock-touching incident." The prosecution argued further that the killing in Thailand bore "striking similarities" to Lowe's murder. All three victims were tourists who went missing soon after meeting Martin.

Their bodies were chopped up and their passports and personal belongings were found on Martin later.

After considering the arguments from both sides, Justice Sinnathuray found that the prosecution was justified in bringing in the Thai evidence. While such evidence would be damaging to his case, Martin was seemingly unbothered as he listened from his cubicle. He looked more bored than frightened at this turn of events.

As the court had approved the admission of the Thai evidence, the statements of Thai witnesses—including Oy LoGate of Nilly's Marina Inn and cab driver Weerasak Wongpanich—and various other documents were brought to the court's attention. All the evidence pointed to the fact that Martin had travelled to Phuket on March 15 on the same flight as the Canadians. They were driven to the same hotel and had also stayed at the same place, in adjacent rooms.

On March 16, Martin moved from his room to the Canadians'. He checked out on March 19 and flew to Singapore, where he was arrested. That same day, Thai police discovered the Canadians' skulls in a disused mine in the Kathu district. Five days later, on March 24, the body parts of Sheila Damude were found in the jungle and on April 3, Thai police found bloodstains in the hotel room occupied by the Canadians.

British forensic scientist Michael John Barber testified that DNA tests showed that the traces of blood on Martin's hammer and the blood found in the Canadians' hotel room were from the same person. While he could not identify this person, those in the courtroom knew he was referring to the probability of the person being Sheila or Darin Damude, both of whom were believed to have been killed by Martin.

Dr Roongrueng Kijphati, the Thai forensic anthropologist who examined the body parts, was also flown in to testify. Unlike the murder of Lowe, in which the cause of death could not be ascertained as the head was missing, Dr Kijphati could say that the probable cause of death of the Canadians was the serious fractures on their skulls.

Speaking through a Thai interpreter, he said the blows could have been caused by Martin's 1.5 kg hammer. The accused's foldable knives could also have been used to cut through the joints as they had sharp points. He noted that the body parts were severed cleanly at the joints by a skilful person without causing damage to the bones. "If they were not done by a doctor, the person must be a butcher. My assistant, who is very skilful and experienced, can do it in five minutes or less."

The boyish-looking doctor added that this was the first time in two years of forensic examinations that he had seen bodies chopped up by an expert. Two years might seem a relatively short time but the doctor was well qualified to make such a remark. He performed autopsies only three days of the week; on each occasion, however, he would see as many as 40 bodies. That meant more than 12,500 bodies in two years.

Singapore's senior forensic pathologist, Prof. Chao Tzee Cheng, was also recalled to comment on the Canadians' body parts. He said Sheila Damude's skull had a fracture on its upper left side. "The force used to hit the skull was so great that the fracture went right to the base of the skull." He agreed with the Thai doctor that this fracture could have been caused by a strong blow from Martin's hammer. As for Darin Damude's skull, the professor said it had fractures in the region of the nose, cheek and eyes, indicating that he was hit by a similarly strong blow on the face.

The prosecution's case ended after six days of hearing, but that was not the end. It had saved its last salvos for Martin should he decide to go on the witness stand.

On October 16, after a five-day break, Justice Sinnathuray ruled that the prosecution had made out a *prima facie* case for a charge of murder and called upon Martin to enter his defence. The accused elected to give oral testimony.

For the first time, a suspected serial killer would speak in an open court in Singapore.

11

TO DISSECT A KILLER

John Martin lost weight in prison. This was due to depression and sleepless nights thinking of the hangman's noose. He was also not used to the Asian-style cooking in prison. He had never eaten so many meals of fried rice in his life. This was what he had during the whole duration of his trial. He used to be heavy-set as he carried weights and worked out, but not any more. He had slimmed down noticeably and looked gaunt.

On October 16, however, he was a confident man. It was his first day in the witness box. He believed he could convince the judge that he did not murder; the killing was unintentional. He painted a sad picture of himself and told a story which was quite different from the police version.

He had left school at 15 because he was suffering from dyslexia and people made fun of him all the time, he said. As he could not study, he helped his widowed mother by working in glass and plastic factories and selling antiques. He became a petty thief but graduated into drug trafficking. He was caught many times and had been in and out of prison. In October 1994, while serving a long sentence for drug trafficking, he absconded during home leave. Using a birth certificate that he had obtained from fellow prisoner Simon James Davis, he made a passport under that name and left England. "I used the assumed name to avoid being detected and arrested for absconding from prison," he said.

After leaving England, he went to several countries and eventually ended up in Mexico. There, he applied for a British passport under his own name, John Martin. He went to Mexico hoping to reconcile with his former wife, Maria. He also wanted to take back all his documents under the names of John Martin and John Martin Scripps. He rented a house in Cancun and lived with Maria and his nine-year-old daughter, Lara. He sold clothes to earn a living.

At about 2 am on March 8, he flew to Singapore. He said he had made prior arrangements to meet his British friend. They would meet in Singapore or Thailand. At the airport, he called a few hotels but they were fully booked. He also tried calling the Raffles Hotel but that was too expensive. In the end, he went to a coffee shop and waited until dawn.

At about 8 am, he went up to hotel reservation clerk Armillah Johar and asked for help in looking for a room. While she was checking, he spoke to the man waiting behind him. He was Gerard George Lowe. Later, when single rooms were still unavailable, they agreed to share a double room. "I am not sure but I believe it was the lady who suggested sharing rooms. I have no problems with sharing rooms with strangers. Also, Mr Lowe seemed friendly. He said he was married and I did not want to spend the whole day looking for a room." He said Armillah offered them a room with a double bed but they said "definitely no!" In the end, they settled for a room with twin beds in River View Hotel.

At the hotel, they were told that their room was not ready, so they decided to go for breakfast. After that, Lowe suggested going to Orchard Road to check the prices of electronic items. "I agreed to follow as, if I had stayed behind, I would just have fallen asleep in the coffee house." In Orchard Road, they went to a number of shops. In one of them, he remembered meeting salesman Danny Teo. He said he wanted to buy computers and intended to pay with the credit card that his bank in San Francisco would send to him in Singapore. Later, they also visited shops in the Raffles City Shopping Centre and a coffee shop before returning to the hotel at midday. They were then given Room 1511.

Inside the room, he said Lowe told him to take a shower first as he looked tired. As he took his towel from the bag, everything fell out, including his clothes and camping equipment. After the shower, he came out wearing only a pair of shorts. He told Mr Lowe he was going to sleep. Just before he fell asleep, he heard Lowe in the shower.

"I was awakened by someone touching my backside. When I turned over, I saw Mr Lowe standing over me, smiling. He had his hand on my backside. I freaked out; I believed the man was going to assault me. So I turned over and kicked him," Martin said.

He told the judge that he was "very nervous" about such things because he had encountered similar experiences in the past. When he was young, he was thrown in a jail in Israel because he could not pay the fines for being drunk and for stealing. In the cell, a fellow prisoner tried to rape him. "I fought with him because I am not a gay and didn't believe in that sort of thing."

He produced a letter from a doctor in Britain which showed that he suffered injuries on his face and arm as a result of the fight. He said he had another similar encounter in a British jail in 1994. He said he was taking a shower when two men came in and tried to rape him. "I ran back to my cell and locked myself in it for two days."

He said after kicking out at Lowe, he started swearing, calling him "a homosexual bastard, a gay and a pouf". He said Lowe fell backwards and hit the dressing table. "He started throwing my things at me. My pouch hit my face and my hammer hit me in the stomach. When I was getting up, Mr Lowe was coming towards me, with his arms out. As I got off the bed, I saw the hammer and picked it up and lashed out in an upward motion. I swung the hammer. The whole incident was very, very short. I later realised that I had hit him because the way he fell made me nervous."

Martin: I did not intend to cause him any serious harm.

Judge: But did you intend to hit the deceased with the hammer?

Martin: No, Your Honour.

After that, he said he dragged Lowe into the bathroom, slumped him over the tub and tried to revive him with running water. "I slapped his face and shook his shoulder. I saw Mr Lowe's chest wasn't moving and I panicked, Your Honour. I just wanted to get out of the hotel as fast as possible. When I saw he was not breathing, I believed I had killed him."

He said he then left the hotel, took a taxi and went to his British friend's hotel. (This, he claimed later, was either The Beaufort Singapore or the Rasa Sentosa Resort.) It was still daylight. "I went to his room; he was in. I told my friend what had happened. My friend couldn't believe what I was telling him. In the end, he asked for my hotel keys and told me to stay in his room and not to open the door to anyone. I stayed in the room until the next morning."

He said his British friend came back late at night. "He said the man was dead but told me not to worry. I asked him why. He told me that he had dumped the body in the river." Later, they had a few drinks. His friend then gave him the dead man's passport and credit card. "My friend said he wanted $12,000 for getting rid of the body. He told me to go to the bank to cash the credit card. He also helped me to change the photograph in Mr Lowe's passport as my hands were shaking too much at that time."

He said he stayed in his friend's hotel until the next day, then returned to his hotel early next morning. He found his pouch missing and went to make a report. The pouch contained traveller's cheques and his passport. He later had coffee with his friend in the hotel opposite his own. After that, they went to the bank in the Raffles City Shopping Centre to withdraw money from Lowe's credit card. "But my friend was not with me in the bank. He remained at a coffee shop in the shopping centre." His friend left after taking $6,000 but he remained in the shopping centre.

"I remembered going into an electrical shop and I bought a VCR for my sister. I did not mean to use Mr Lowe's credit card to pay for it. The card was in my wallet when I took it out to pay. The salesman saw the card and said that they would take credit cards."

He said he met his British friend again the next day as the man wanted him to withdraw more money. "I recalled going to the bank to withdraw more money to get my friend off my back." He said that during this time, he could not think straight. "I have never done anything like this before in my life. I could not sleep as I kept dreaming about the man in the bath." He said he decided to go to Thailand as he needed time to sort out his problem. "I arranged to meet my friend there as I told him that I could not handle this any more."

Martin remained vague about his time in Thailand. He said he recalled meeting the Canadians. They shared a taxi to the hotel but he did not meet them after that. He only found out about their murders after his arrest by the Singapore police. The belongings of the Canadians were given to him by his British friend, he said. The man also handed their passports to him but he could not recognise their photographs at the time.

The defence lawyer closed his case by asking Martin questions about Lowe.

Counsel: When you were holding the hammer, did you have the intention to cause harm to him?

Martin: No. I just wanted to keep him away. I did not intentionally want to harm him. By nature, I am not violent. My history will show you that I am not a violent person.

Counsel: Did you have anything to do with the disarticulation of the deceased's body?

Martin: No. I believed my friend must have done it but I did not know how he cut it up.

The final question from counsel was, "Who is this British friend?" In an emotional voice, Martin replied, "I have said that I am unable to tell the police because it will involve my family. He is involved with people who deal in drugs. If I reveal his name, my family and I will be killed. I have no doubts about that. Once they killed the wife and baby of this man even though they were under police protection. They used the car and ran them over and over again. I know what they are capable of."

To the prosecution, this was merely a fine piece of acting. The emotional touch during the last scene was commendable, but the prosecution was not taken in easily. It wanted to show that Martin was the lone killer and the British friend did not exist. The man was merely a fictitious character cooked up by Martin to cover up his own misdeeds. To prove this, the killer had to be dissected first.

To find loopholes in his lie, the DPP took him 10 years back in time and asked him how he got to know his British friend. Martin confidently told his story. He said he knew the man through the man's brother, who was a good friend of his. While he was in and out of British jails for burglary and drug offences between 1985 and 1994, he said the friend visited him. Apart from his own mother and sister, other friends who had visited him were "Rupert, Jesse and Colin". The British friend was in his 40s. He was not a small-time drug dealer and had connections in Europe. "Other members of his family are also involved in drugs, but not his mother." He refused to divulge the friend's name, address or telephone number. "Such information may assist me in this proceeding but it will cause the death of my family. I do not want this to happen."

He also took care not to keep a written record of such information because he did not want it to fall into the hands of the police. Instead, he noted the information on a piece of paper and gave it to someone whom he trusted. Whenever he wanted to contact his British friend, he would call this person first, he said.

DPP: What is the name of this person?

Martin: If I give you his name, I might as well give you my friend's name.

Judge: What about his first name? You can't identify anyone with that. It can be Tom, Dick or Harry.

Martin: I'd rather not say, Your Honour.

Upon further probing, he admitted that the person who

kept his British friend's telephone number was "Colin". For good measure, he added, "Colin was a close friend but we have since drifted apart. I have Colin's telephone number but I did not write it down in my diary. It is the only number which I can remember because the numbers are easy to remember."

DPP: What is the number then?

Martin: If I give you the number, you can locate his name and address. You can then get the other information as well.

Martin said that before he came to Singapore on March 8, he had called his British friend from San Francisco to make arrangements to meet. They were to meet in Singapore or Bangkok. He said his friend gave him the names of two hotels in each of the cities. He wrote this on a piece of paper. He added that his friend was also travelling under an assumed name, using another man's passport. "I can't give you his assumed name because you can then look for this person and police will be able to find my friend. Just like when police went to look for Simon Davis, he immediately gave details about me."

DPP: You kept many things and receipts with you. But the piece of paper which had your friend's hotels was not found on you. What happened to it?

Martin: I threw the paper away in Bangkok as it grew tatty.

DPP: Did you meet your friend in Thailand?

Martin: I saw him every day while in Phuket. We had arranged to meet in Bangkok. He came later to meet me because I said I was going to Phuket. But we never travelled on the same plane.

DPP: Why? Are you afraid of a plane crash?

Martin: No. More afraid of being arrested together.

When asked why he returned to Singapore on March 19, Martin said his original plan, before he killed Lowe, was to return to Singapore after Thailand and then fly back to Mexico. "If you caused death in a country, you will not go back to that country. I was confused at that time. Half of me wanted to come back to Singapore while the other half wanted to go to Mexico."

Judge: Why do you want to come back knowing that you had killed Mr Lowe?

Martin: I don't know. I just wasn't thinking straight.

While he avoided giving a direct answer, it was obvious to the prosecution that Martin returned to Singapore because he had not counted on being arrested. He thought the victim's identity was still a mystery to the Singapore police.

The prosecution's attacks began to leave their mark. Martin started losing his grip on the story built around his British friend. His confidence was badly shaken after a day of intense questioning. He began to clamp up and become more cautious. Initially, he had to be told by his lawyer and the judge to answer the questions and stop rambling. Now, his constant refrain became "I don't know", "I can't remember" and "I am not sure", so much so that everyone in the courtroom could almost always predict his reply. He defended his instant amnesia by reminding his audience regularly that he had a poor memory due to dyslexia. This was worsened by his drinking and taking Valium. The net effect was that he was either drunk or "stoned and drunk" most of the time.

The battering continued when the prosecution wanted to probe how he managed to lay his hands on the green backpack which belonged to Darin Damude.

DPP: How did the green backpack come into your possession?

Martin: My friend gave it to me. I had the bag when I changed my hotel room.

DPP: Did you bring the green backpack to Room 43?

Martin: I can't remember.

DPP: Did you have the green backpack when you were in Room 43?

Martin: I am not sure. When my friend was there, the green bag was there.

DPP: But who took the bag to Room 43?

Martin: I can't remember which items I had brought along when I moved room.

DPP: If you cannot be specific, say so.

Martin lost his cool and retorted, "You asked a specific question, I cannot give you a specific answer. I am unable to do so because I can't remember. I was confused by your cross-examination. You were asking me questions about things which happened some time ago when I was stone drunk. I am confused myself. I can't even remember the room number. How the bag was in the room, I can't remember. I am unsure if my friend brought it with him when he visited me or if he gave it to me in Bangkok. The bag was given to me somehow. I am not sure how."

In his statement to the police earlier, Martin had also said that his British friend gave him the green backpack in Bangkok. The only problem with this answer was that the scenario he set out could never have happened. Darin Damude was still alive in Bangkok and had flown together with him to Phuket. The careless answer indicated that Martin was losing track of the lie he had concocted.

He was then asked how he got Sheila Damude's floral bag. He said his British friend brought the bag to his hotel room on March 17. He claimed the friend opened the bag and looked through the things. He later asked Martin to throw the bag and its contents away.

Martin: I can't remember whether he had taken anything. When he was going through the things, I was at the balcony. Even if I had seen it, I can't remember it now.

DPP: Did you ask your friend why couldn't he get rid of the bag himself?

Martin: I can't remember.

DPP: Don't you think it was rather odd that he checked it and then asked you to get rid of it?

Martin: It is normal to me.

DPP: Why then did you not get rid of the bag?

Martin: I looked at it and it was in quite a good condition. It would be a shame to throw it into the rubbish.

DPP: Did you go through the things?
Martin: I can't remember.

At this point, the judge interrupted the prosecutor and posed a question to Martin.

Judge: Mr Martin, you keep saying "I can't remember." I ask myself this question, "How did you remember your friend handing the bag to you to get rid of it?" If you cannot remember so many things, why did you remember him giving it to you? Did it really happen?
Martin: Yes, Your Honour. But I can't remember the details.

The focus then fell on the Canadians'belongings, especially their passports, credit cards and traveller's cheques. Martin said all these were given to him by his British friend when he went to his friend's hotel room one night. The friend even glued Martin's photographs over those of the Canadians and told him to forge the signatures so that he could use their credit cards and traveller's cheques. Martin said he followed the man's instructions because he was indebted to him.

Martin: I remember practising the signatures but I can't remember if those were their signatures.
DPP: Why can't you remember?
Martin: I was drunk then.

The DPP then referred Martin to a memo pad on which he had practised the Canadians' signatures and asked how he could write neat and similar signatures if he was drunk.

Martin replied, "Normally, when I sign, my signature

varies a lot. But because I was drunk, I was able to do it so neatly and precisely, if that makes any sense to you."

The DPP was flabbergasted. She paused for several seconds before resuming her questioning.

The attention then focused on events that took place in Singapore on March 9, a day after Lowe was killed. Martin said that upon returning to his hotel room, he discovered that his pouch, which contained his passport and traveller's cheques, was missing. He then went to the hotel reception counter to obtain Thomas Cook's telephone number so he could report the lost cheques. He also called his friend at the lobby and then returned to his room.

The DPP countered, "But just the other day, you testified that you first called Thomas Cook in the UK, went to the lobby to call your friend and then to the reception. So which is it now?"

Martin was caught lying because he had forgotten his own testimony. But he said, "I am telling the same things. One may be out of sequence but both are the same. You've got good memory, I haven't. I am dyslexic. If you give me three things to remember, by the third time, I would have gotten it all mixed up."

The first damning documentary evidence came on the tenth day of the trial. The prosecution produced a receipt from River View Hotel's River Garden Restaurant which was supposedly signed by a Mr Davis from Room 1511 at 9.28 pm on March 8. The time and date were crucial because Martin had said that during that time, he was seeking refuge in his British friend's hotel after he killed the South African. If the prosecution could show that he had indeed signed the bill, it would show that he had lied about his whereabouts that night. This was also a very strong piece of evidence to show that Martin's "friend" was an imaginary one.

DPP: Did you have a meal at the hotel on the night of March 8?

Martin: No.

DPP: But you signed the bill. It stated that you had a fillet steak and also a glass of white wine.

Martin: Fillet steak with white wine? It couldn't be me.

DPP: Why? Are you a vegetarian?

Martin: No. Because if I have red meat, I always have red wine.

Martin continued to deny that he was in the restaurant at that time. He said the signature on the bill was not his. How could he sign the bill if he was at his friend's hotel, he argued. He suggested to the court that his friend could have ordered the meal. After all, the man went to the hotel to help him dispose of Lowe's body. Maybe the friend felt hungry after all the hard work.

The prosecution then produced a Department of Scientific Services report which detailed a test to compare the signature on the bill with Martin's specimen signatures given to the police while he was in prison. The expert who conducted the test was Ng Gek Kwee, a senior document examiner with 20 years' experience. She had attended relevant courses at Scotland Yard in Britain and at the Secret Services and Federal Bureau of Investigation in the United States. Due to significant similarities between the signature on the bill and Martin's own signature, she did not have any doubt that Martin had, in fact, signed the bill. In spite of what the expert said, Martin insisted that he was not the one. He said he often signed "Davis" with a "J." in front, and this was not on the bill.

He asked the DPP, "But did any witness in the coffee shop identify me?"

The judge said, "This is something that you should tell your lawyer instead."

The judge continued, "As the trial judge and the trier of facts, I wish to point out to you that the unchallenged evidence produced by the learned deputy is totally against your testimony that you were not at the hotel that day. Do you see this?"

Martin replied, "I don't know, Your Honour. It was not my signature."

The DPP next asked Martin why he went to the hotel reception on the morning of March 9 to ask the staff to delete Lowe's name from the register.

Martin said, "Because he was no longer staying there. He was in the river. I do not know what I was thinking then."

The prosecution then moved in for another kill. It produced a used ticket stub and a programme book for the Singapore Symphony Orchestra's classical music concert playing at the Victoria Concert Hall on the night of March 10. The items were found among Martin's belongings at the time of his arrest. He had claimed earlier that he was drinking with his British friend at the man's hotel that night, but the documentary evidence showed otherwise. How could he be with his friend when he was at the concert? That night's programme had included Tchaikovsky's Symphony No. 6 and Brahms' Piano Concerto No. 1.

Martin: I didn't go to the concert, Your Honour.

DPP: But the used ticket and programme book were seized from you?

Martin: I don't like classical music. I go to rock concerts.

DPP: I am suggesting to you that the used ticket and programme book were proof that you attended the concert at about 8.15 pm on March 10.

Martin: No. I would remember going to something like a concert. I am sure I did not go. I was drinking with my friend.

The questioning then turned to his 1.5 kg "camping" hammer. He said he last saw it when he dropped it on the bed after hitting Lowe in the hotel room. His friend might have taken it when he went to the room to get rid of Lowe's body. Martin said he only saw it again after he was arrested by the police. When asked by the DPP, he said he did not see the hammer even though he packed his bag before he left Singapore on March 11.

He said, "I would definitely remember if I saw it. Ever since the incident, there were recurrences of what had happened in my mind and the hammer was always there."

Under cross-examination, Martin admitted that he learnt butchery skills while he was in prison in Britain.

Martin: I was a qualified butcher but only limited in

certain things. I am not a skilled butcher.

DPP: Do you agree that you need a short, sharp knife to cut at the joint?

Martin: Yes. A boning knife is sharp at the end. No need to be a large knife.

DPP: What about a serrated knife, about four inches long?

Martin: In butchery, I only used a straight knife.

DPP: But Mr James Quigley said a serrated knife can also be used.

Martin: He knows more about knives than I do.

DPP: How long would you take to bone out the quarters of beef?

Martin: It would take me a day to take out the bones.

DPP: But Mr Quigley said it would take only few minutes.

Martin: If you are very skilful, yes.

DPP: Would you agree that whatever skills you picked up as a butcher can be used to disarticulate a human?

Martin: From the photographs, when I looked at some of the bones, they looked similar to those of an animal. But other parts, no.

DPP: Would you agree that it would not take more than three hours to disarticulate a human, for a person who was reasonably skilled?

Martin: I don't know. I can't be sure whether it was done skilfully. I feel very sick when I looked at the photographs of the parts.

DPP: I put it to you that you had the butchery skills and it was you who had disarticulated Mr Lowe sometime on March 8 at the River View Hotel.

Martin: No. I didn't have all the skills which the lady mentioned, Your Honour.
DPP: But you had the tools to do it.
Martin: Yes.
DPP: You had ample time to kill, disarticulate and to pack his body parts.
Martin: I killed the man, yes. But after that incident, I went to my friend's hotel.
DPP: I put it to you that you did all these between noon and 5 pm on March 8.
Martin: No.
DPP: After this, you met Danny Teo at his shop.
Martin: That was in the morning. No, not true.
DPP: You had ample opportunities to throw the parts into the Singapore River.
Martin: No. I didn't do that.

He then pushed the blame of cutting up Lowe's body to his British friend.

DPP: How long have you known your friend?
Martin: Eight to 10 years.
DPP: How old is he?
Martin: Older than me. I know his brother better. I know he does drugs. I think he has also worked in a slaughterhouse before.

Suddenly, the man who was supposed to be a drug kingpin also knew butchery.

DPP: I put it to you that all these, including your British friend, were a fabrication.

Martin: I wish it was.

If it was true that his friend had disposed of the body, Martin was asked how the man had carried it out of the hotel without anyone noticing. He said, "I can't remember him giving me a clear explanation about this. It seemed odd to me that he could take out the body when there were so many people at the lobby. I remembered asking him about this but he did not give a clear answer. He did not want to talk about it. He always clamped up. I asked him whether he threw it into the river behind the hotel and he did not even say that."

The prosecution again returned to events leading to the death of Lowe. Topics of cross-examination were not presented chronologically but in a chaotic manner. This was a tactic used to confuse Martin, so that he could be caught lying by giving inconsistent answers to the same questions.

DPP: If your intention was to keep Mr Lowe away, could you not use your hands to restrain him?

Martin: It happened so fast. If I had time to think, I would not be sitting in this courtroom. I have often walked away from violence.

DPP: When he touched your buttocks, could he have intended to just wake you up?

Martin: No normal man would touch the backside to wake up a person.

DPP: But there was nothing in his conduct which suggested that he intended to sexually assault you against your will.

Martin: It didn't seem like that to me. Another man was touching my backside. It was not normal. I freaked out. I don't know whether touching the backside is an offence here but from where I come, it is.

DPP: Why did you react that way?

Martin: It was not just a touch. His whole hand was on my backside.

If the killing had occurred accidentally after an attempted sexual attack, why didn't Martin report the matter to the police?

He said, "Because I killed a man. The man died in my hands. What I understood about Singapore law then was that you get an automatic death sentence. My first thought was to get away. I washed away the blood from my hands, changed quickly and went downstairs. At that time, I just wanted to get out of the hotel."

DPP: Did you give any thought to Mr Lowe who was in the bathroom?

Martin: Afterwards, yes, but not at that time.

DPP: If you were dazed, confused and shocked at that time, why did you remember to take your wallet with you?

Martin: I don't know what I was thinking at that time.

DPP: Why did you want to get out of the room?

Martin: I just didn't want to stay in the room. I thought about my friend and I just wanted to get to his hotel.

DPP: You have testified that you met your friend at places such as his hotel, opposite your hotel, in the Raffles City Shopping Centre and in the hotel in Marina

Square. But in your statement to the police, you said that you only met him in Orchard Road.

Martin: That statement was not true. I lied.

He was then asked about events in Phuket. Again, he remained vague. He admitted arriving at Nilly's Marina Inn together with the Canadians but after that, he said, they did not have any more contact. He said that soon after checking into his room, he went to the beach where he sat down and had drinks until it was dark. "I had several drinks but I can't recall how many. I remembered having a drink with fruits and an umbrella in it."

He added that he went for a long walk later before returning to his room to sleep. The next morning, he was informed by the hotel that he could change his room, as he had earlier asked for a room with a sea view. He said he only realised that he was moving to the Canadians' room, which was next to his, when he went to collect his things. When the judge asked whether this would have made him curious about the Canadians' whereabouts, he replied coldly, "I gave no thought to it."

The defence's case was drawing to an end. Martin had been in the witness box for eight days. The time had come for the prosecution to confront him with point-blank questions. His story about the sexual attack was untrue. The fact was that Martin killed Lowe intentionally because he wanted to rob him. This was also the reason for killing the Canadians. To cover up, he cooked up an incredible tale and also created a British friend to take the rap. He said things that he wanted the court to hear. In addressing other things that he could not explain as they would implicate him, he said he could not remember or was drunk. Martin denied all the charges vehemently. He even retorted, "If I had made up my British friend, I would have said that he killed Mr Lowe and not me."

He maintained that he did not kill the Canadians and that he killed Lowe unintentionally. Before he finally left the witness box, he gave a solemn parting shot: "That incident should not have happened. I am very sorry to the sister and wife for having to go to the morgue to identify his parts. No one should have gone through this."

However his troubles were far from over as the prosecution had one last deadly blow. At the eleventh hour, it applied for another crucial piece of evidence to be admitted to shoot down Martin's tale about his British friend.

He had said earlier that this man had stayed at either The Beaufort Singapore or Shangri-La's Rasa Sentosa Resort, but had refused to be specific. He claimed that the friend moved to another hotel in the Marina Square Shopping Mall on March 10. The mall had three adjoining hotels: Marina Mandarin, Oriental and Pan Pacific. Again, he refused to say which of the three hotels his friend had stayed in. He said that his friend had checked in with another person's passport but refused to disclose his friend's assumed name or nationality.

The police wanted to prove that the man did not exist. The only way to do this was to approach all the hotels for help. But time was running out. While the lawyers were fighting the case in court, ASP Gerald Lim and Staff Sgt

Zainal Abidin had to work hard to gather this last bit of evidence. By this time, another experienced investigator, Inspector Zainudin Lee, had joined the body parts murder squad. Together, they went to all five hotels and asked for the names of all single male guests who had checked in or out of the hotels on March 10.

Such information was important because if the British friend really existed, his name or assumed name would be on the guest lists. The officers' finding showed that about 150 single male guests of various nationalities had checked out of the two hotels in Sentosa on March 10. But when they cross-checked these names one by one against the names on the March 10 check-in registers of the three hotels in Marina Square, they found no matches. If the British friend really existed, his name should be found on the lists of the Sentosa hotels and again on the lists of the Marina Square hotels. But it was not, and this showed that Martin was lying.

But what if the friend had carried two different passports and used different names at the hotels? If that were so, the officers' checks would not be useful. But, in reality, why would the friend use different assumed names for something as innocuous as checking into hotels? Martin, a fugitive on the run, did not use two different names himself when he was in Singapore.

12

DEATH OF A KILLER

John Martin was a calculating killer who had no qualms about lying to exonerate himself from the murder charge. This was the thrust of the prosecution's case at the end of the trial. In her closing speech, DPP Jennifer Marie said that the motive for the murder of Gerard George Lowe was robbery. "It is more than a coincidence that the accused had, on March 11, actually remitted the sum of S$8,500 to his Citibank account in the United States." S$8,400 was the amount he had withdrawn from Lowe's credit card. After the killing, he bought things for himself and his sister, attended a concert and talked about collecting coins. This was a far cry from the picture he had painted of himself: that of a confused, dazed man walking in a dream world.

In what was perhaps the most convincing argument of the case, the DPP referred to the killings of Lowe and the Canadians as "hallmark crimes". The conservative term was used by the English courts to refer to what is known in the United States as "serial killing". For the first time in a Singapore court, an accused was being branded a serial killer. This was because Martin's crimes had telltale signs that were so similar, they became as personal as his own fingerprints.

SIMILARITIES IN THE KILLINGS

SINGAPORE	THAILAND
1. Martin met Lowe at Changi International Airport on March 8. They shared a taxi to the River View Hotel.	1. Martin met the Damudes at Phuket Airport on March 15. They shared a taxi to Nilly's Marina Inn.
2. They checked into the same room. Martin asked the hotel to cancel Lowe's name the next day.	2. They stayed in adjacent rooms. Martin moved into the Damudes' room the next day.
3. Martin said he killed Lowe by hitting his head with a hammer.	3. The skulls of the Damudes had serious fractures caused by a hammer.
4. Lowe's body was cut expertly at the joints before disposal.	4. The Damudes' bodies were cut expertly at the joints before disposal.
5. There were bloodstains in Lowe's hotel room.	5. There were bloodstains in the Damudes' hotel room.
6. Martin kept Lowe's passports, credit cards and other belongings.	6. Martin kept the Damudes' passports, credit cards and other belongings.
7. Martin forged Lowe's signatures.	7. Martin forged the Damudes' signatures
8. Martin's photograph was affixed to Lowe's passport.	8. Martin's photographs were affixed to the Damudes' passports.

To support its case, the prosecution cited the cases of convicted serial murderers in England. One of them was the famous English "Brides in the Bath" case in 1915, in which George Smith was charged with murdering his wife. He claimed that she had drowned in a bathtub during an epileptic fit but the Crown led evidence to show that two of his other wives had died in a similar fashion. Each time, Smith stood to gain financially from the death. The British Court of Criminal Appeal supported the use of earlier cases to convict Smith and sentenced him to hang.

In his judgment, Lord Reid said, "If you find an accident which benefits a person and you find that the person has been sufficiently fortunate to have an accident happen to him a number of times, benefiting him each time, you draw a very strong, frequently irresistible inference that the occurrence of so many accidents, benefiting him in such a coincidence, cannot have happened unless it was a design."

On November 10, 1995, after a 16-day trial, the Singapore High Court returned a guilty verdict. John Martin's fate was sealed.

Justice T.S. Sinnathuray said, "Having taken time to consider, I have, during this adjournment, carefully reviewed the evidence given in this trial and studied the submissions made in this case. As Martin has admitted that he killed Lowe, the issue I have to decide is not whether he is guilty or innocent of the charge for which he was tried, but whether he is guilty of murder or of culpable homicide not amounting to murder.

"Suffice it to say that I do not accept the evidence of Martin that there was a sudden fight in Room 1511 at the River View Hotel on March 8, 1995. I also altogether reject his evidence that he had a British friend in Singapore at that time who disposed of the body of Lowe for him. On the totality of the evidence before me, I am satisfied beyond reasonable doubt that Martin had intentionally killed Lowe; after that he disarticulated Lowe's body into separate parts and it was he who subsequently disposed of the body parts by throwing them into the river behind the hotel. I have come to this decision independently of the Thai evidence.

"I now turn to the Thai evidence. Martin in his testimony was generally evasive and unable to give a consistent and believable account of his stay in Phuket. Specifically, the evidence about his movements the day when he had checked in at the hotel was unreliable. His evidence was even more incredible when it came for him to explain how the bags belonging to Sheila and Darin and their personal effects came into his possession. It would have been clear to anyone who heard his explanations that the British friend whom he said had given him all those things was a figment of his imagination. On the evidence, I had no difficulty to find that it was Martin who was concerned with the deaths of Sheila and Darin and for the disposal of their body parts found in different sites in Phuket.

"I accept the written submissions of the learned DPPs, which Ms Jennifer Marie summarised in court, that there are striking similarities which cannot be merely coincidental relating to the deaths of Lowe in Singapore and Sheila and Darin in Thailand. The disarticulation of the body parts of Lowe, Sheila and Darin have the hallmark signs of having been done by the same person.

"The Thai evidence is materially relevant in the present case because this evidence rebuts Martin's defence that there was a sudden fight between him and Lowe and that he did not kill him intentionally.

"In addition, though it was submitted by Mr Edmond Pereira that the Thai evidence was prejudicial to Martin, in the present case, I am of the view that the probative value of this evidence far outweighs its prejudicial effect. Altogether, this similar fact evidence reinforces the decision I have made, for it puts beyond doubt that Martin is guilty on the charge of murder.

"Accordingly, I find Martin guilty and convict him on the charge."

After Justice Sinnathuray gave his judgment, the court clerk asked all who were present in court to stand for the death sentence to be passed. Martin stood up and looked at the judge. He was stony-faced and expressionless. The judge said to him, "You will be taken from this place to a lawful prison and place of execution where you will be hanged by the neck until you are dead. May the Lord have mercy on your soul."

Martin was led out of the courtroom immediately after the session was over. He would be placed in a cell in Changi Prison's Death Row until his execution. He was a condemned man.

A couple of days later, he filed an appeal against his

conviction. Under the law, a person who faces the death penalty is entitled to present his case to the Court of Appeal. However, on January 5, 1996, Martin met his lawyer, Joseph Theseira, and signed documents indicating that he wished to drop the appeal. The body parts serial murderer was resigned to his fate and ready to accept his retribution.

Several weeks later, he also wrote a letter to the President of Singapore, indicating that he did not wish to appeal for a pardon against the death sentence. He wanted to end it all quickly, not wanting to prolong his stay in prison.

He was finally led to the gallows and executed at dawn on April 19, 1996. It was a Friday morning. On the same day, the Thai police closed their files on the murders of Canadians Sheila and Darin Damude.

13

PROFILE OF A SERIAL KILLER

"Serial killing" is a relatively new term in the area of police investigation. It refers to a series of murders committed by the same killer. Usually, all the murders bear similarities that can be viewed as the killer's distinct trademark. In the late 1970s, such crimes were called "stranger killings" because, in most cases, the perpetrators did not know their victims.

For example, David Berkowitz, better known as Son of Sam, terrorised New York in 1977 when he hunted courting couples and lone women for no apparent reason. He was credited with six murders. It would have been 13 if seven of his other victims did not survive.

The term "stranger killers" was dropped from use later as law enforcers found it inaccurate. In certain cases, the killers knew their victims. "Serial killers" became the common term instead, a word coined by retired Federal Bureau of Investigation veteran Robert K. Ressler. His work at the Behavioral Science Unit had inspired the popular novel and movie, *Silence of the Lambs*. In real life, part of Ressler's work involved interviewing actual serial killers, such as Berkowitz, Ted Bundy, John Wayne Gacy, Edward Kemper and Jeffrey Dahmer. He talked to them to gain an insight into the workings of their minds, to determine what it was that drove them to kill. More importantly, such experience enabled him to draw astonishingly accurate descriptions of other unidentified serial killers. This invaluable tool, which has helped the police to track down killers, is known as criminal profiling.

According to general profiles, serial killers are usually white males in their 20s or 30s. Their victims are also white as they seldom chose those outside their own kind. There were basically two types of serial killers: the organised and the disorganised.

As the term suggests, a disorganised killer usually leaves several clues at the scene. He does not bother to hide his victim's body which, in most cases, has been mutilated. Usually, these killers have serious psychological problems; they do not bother much about themselves and this can lead to an unkempt physical appearance. Their choice of victims can be rather illogical and the act of killing may be carried out on the spur of the moment without any planning. One such killer, who entered his victims' houses to kill, said his choice very much depended on whether the door was locked. If it was, it meant that the owner did not welcome him and he would go to another house.

Murders committed by an organised killer, on the other hand, are usually premeditated. He first hatches a plan to control, gain the confidence of or get near his victims. Once this is done, he moves in for the kill. In most cases, the killer does not leave any obvious clues behind, such as fingerprints, which will put the police on his trail. Another characteristic is that the killer usually takes the personal items of his victims as "trophies". In doing so, the killer creates a further problem for the police as the removal of personal belongings may hamper the initial identification of the victim.

Arguably, John Martin was an organised serial killer. He was 35 and white. All his victims were also white; he came into close contact with Asians in Singapore and Thailand but did not kill any of them. His murders were committed in a similar fashion. He planned the killings well and later took pains to dispose of the bodies. He also kept his victims' belongings, and these included the clothes of the female victim. But the biggest distinction between him and the other serial killers was that his crimes were not motivated by sex; his primary intention was to get more money.

It may also be argued that he did not derive pleasure from the act of killing itself, unlike some other killers. His satisfaction probably came afterwards, when he finally got hold of his victims' money. Martin, however, outclassed others when it came to the disposal of the bodies. Not many killers could claim that they had skilfully dismembered a human body.

So what drove Martin to commit such a brutal act? The transformation of an ordinary person into a serial killer does not happen overnight. Problems which cause people to kill are usually deep-rooted and take many years to develop before they get out of hand. And the killings usually take place after certain events "trigger" the killer's basic instincts.

John Martin Scripps was born in Hertfortshire, England, on December 9, 1959. He was the younger child of an East End trucker and a Fleet Street barmaid. He had an elder sister who was five years older.

As a boy, he travelled widely and visited countries in Europe and Asia. He was very close to his father, who accompanied him on some of these trips. Everything went well until he was 10 and his father died suddenly. Martin told the Singapore police, "I do not know how he died. Nevertheless, his death shocked me and this was how I acquired my present problems of reading and writing." In his dyslexic condition, he found it difficult to cope with schoolwork and his classmates taunted him. He avoided them, became a loner and left school at the age of 15.

He took on odd jobs in factories and sold antiques on the streets, but he did not give up his interest in travelling. He worked hard and used his savings to travel. While abroad, he worked at various jobs and sold antiques to pay for his trips.

In May 1974, at the age of 16, he was involved in burglary, caught and brought before the Highgate Juvenile Court. As it was his first offence, he was given a 12-month conditional discharge and fined £10. But he did not repent. In November that same year, he was charged again with burglary, fined £5 and put on a two-year probation. In February the following year, he was caught in the act of breaking in, fined £6 and received a further supervision order. But that still did not deter him. In August 1976, he was caught stealing meat and put on a two-year supervision order.

In June 1978, at the age of 19, he pushed a girl to the ground, lay on top of her and fondled her breasts. As he was no longer a juvenile, the Hendon Magistrates Court slapped a £40 fine on him for indecent assault.

That incident seemed to have kept the young Martin away from trouble for a while and he continued travelling. In 1980, during one of his trips to Montreal, Canada, he met a Mexican girl, Maria. After a whirlwind romance, he took her back to London, where they were married. He was then 21 and she, 17.

Things went well for two years until he returned to his old ways. In October 1982, he was charged with 10 counts of theft and burglary. The total value of property involved was £30,000. He also assaulted police constables when he resisted arrest. The Kingston Crown Court passed a three-year jail sentence on him. This incident affected his relationship with Maria, who was disappointed with him for breaking his promise to stay away from crime. Apparently, she also discovered that he was seeing another woman.

In June 1985, he was in trouble again. He had not completed his jail term but was on home leave when he absconded and committed burglary. For that, he was sentenced to another three years in jail. While he served time in prison, Maria filed for divorce.

Maria later fell in love with a policeman with the elite

bodyguards of the British Royal Family. Martin heard about Maria's boyfriend while he was in prison. One night, while on home leave, he went to look for her and banged on her door. When she opened it, he grabbed hold of her, choked her and, in a fit of anger, threatened to kill her boyfriend. Later, he cried and pleaded with her to take him back. Maria took a day to calm him down; she said she would continue to see him provided he did not harm her boyfriend.

However, when Martin went back to prison, she married her boyfriend. He was devastated and reportedly asked his cellmate, a drug offender, to "bump off" the policeman for marrying his ex-wife. The cellmate, however, dismissed the plan as crazy. Later, during another round of home leave, Martin went to the couple's house in North London intending to cause trouble, but the policeman was away on duty. He stole some of the man's clothes as a way of taking revenge on him. He was appeased only after Maria filed for a divorce from the British policeman and returned to her hometown in Cancun, Mexico.

After his release from prison, one of the first things he did was to change his name legally to John Martin. Apparently, this was his way of signalling a new start in life. He did not return to burglary but became involved in drugs instead. As he was an experienced traveller, he worked as a courier for a drug syndicate and carried heroin between Asia and Europe. During one of his drug runs in 1987, he came to Singapore and stashed away 1.5 kg of heroin in the safe deposit box of a bank in Orchard Road. He kept it there because the goods cost close to US$1 million. He had never possessed so much money in his life and losing the drugs would be unthinkable.

His activities were exposed later when he was arrested at London's Heathrow Airport for the possession of drugs. The safebox key was found on him and this led Singapore's Central Narcotics Bureau to the heroin.

One might say it was fortunate for Martin that he was arrested in London. If he had been caught in Singapore, the subsequent body parts murders would never have taken place. Under Singapore law, trafficking in more than 15 g of heroin carries the mandatory death penalty.

In January 1988, the Southwark Crown Court jailed him seven years for the drug offences and £5,000 in drug money was seized. Martin, however, was a recalcitrant criminal. He absconded again during home leave and was involved in drugs again and rearrested. In July 1992, the Winchester Crown Court sentenced him to another six years in jail. If there were no remission for good conduct, Martin would have remained in prison until the year 2001.

One of the key events which eventually transformed Martin into a cold-blooded killer took place during this stint in prison. In 1993, he was found to be a model prisoner and promoted from menial worker to butcher. He was taught how to use knives and assigned to work in the butchery department. Every day, he did nothing but cut meat up. He worked alone and there was no one to talk to. This went on for six months.

Such intense pressure would be intolerable for any man let alone Martin, who had a troubled childhood. He might not be psychotic as there was no evidence to suggest this but one thing was certain: the prolonged exposure could have caused him to become immune to the sight of carcasses and blood. This could explain why he could cut up the bodies of the South African and Canadians without any remorse or fear. To him, it was just another day in the butchery department.

In October 1994, he planned to abscond from prison again. Before his scheduled home leave at the end of the month, he sold his belongings, including his television and video recorder. This was a clear indication that he would not return but the authorities did not suspect anything and allowed him to leave.

After his escape from Britain, he went to look for Maria in Mexico. By then, she already had a nine-year-old daughter, Lara, whom he thought was fathered by the British policeman. In his statement to the Singapore police, he said, "I met Maria there and she told me that her daughter was actually mine and not the British police officer's. I believed her as she was the only woman I had ever loved. Moreover, she explained that she got pregnant during one of my home leave stints from prison, during which time she was already seeing the British officer. After that, we reconciled our relationship."

Although that could be his intention, Maria's own plans were different; she was seeing another man. He begged her to leave her new boyfriend but she refused. Despite the uneasiness which existed between them, Martin was happy to play a doting father to Lara.

During this period, he wrote notes in his diary, found

among his possessions in Singapore. The notes were short, possibly because, being dyslexic, he was poor in the use of language and spelling. Between December 18, 1994, and January 13, 1995, his entries referred mostly to Maria and Lara. For example, on December 18, he wrote "See Maria at mothers." On December 20, it was "Go to the Piramides (Pyramids) with Lara." Maria was apparently unhappy that Martin was spending too much time with Lara. On December 22, Martin wrote "Go to the funfare with Lara. Good day but Pilar monde at me for being lat with Lara." What he had probably meant was "Pilar mad at me for being late with Lara." Pilar was Maria's middle name.

The most revealing entry was probably the one which he wrote on January 12, 1995. By then, something must have happened to Martin and this event possibly transformed him into a killer. He was clearly disturbed when he wrote, "Go to Belize for wot? Today to make money." It was suggested that things were not going well between Martin and Maria. He might have wanted to prove to her that he was not useless and could make lots of money. Not long after that, 28-year-old Briton Timothy McDowell disappeared while holidaying in Belize.

Scotland Yard officers believed that McDowell was also a victim of Martin's. It was not known how the Cambridge graduate, who worked as a management consultant in a packaging firm, came to be associated with Martin. There were no witnesses to the suspected murder. Police believed that after McDowell was killed, his body was thrown into a crocodile-infested river. The strongest evidence linking Martin to the crime was the fact that about US$30,000 was moved from McDowell's bank account to Martin's account in Britain and, later, to the United States.

Martin had denied having anything to do with McDowell's disappearance. After his conviction in Singapore for the murder of South African tourist Gerard George Lowe, he refused to see Scotland Yard officers who wanted to interview him in Changi Prison's Death Row. He kept the answer to McDowell's fate with him right till the end.

There was one factor which supported Scotland Yard's theory. Experts have said that organised serial killers get better after each killing. They learn from their own mistakes so that subsequent killings would be more perfect, with fewer clues left behind. This is why certain mass murderers, such as Ted Bundy, can go free to commit more murders before they are finally arrested. The killing of Lowe in Singapore demonstrated a high degree of skill in planning and disposal of the body and other evidence. This is a good indication that the killing might not have been Martin's first.

Finally, it is noteworthy that, while all attention focused on Martin and his victims during police investigations and the subsequent trial, there were two men who escaped public notice but deserve special mention. This is because they could be dead now if they had not escaped Martin's clutches.

The first man is Jim Steiner. His credit card was found

on Martin but he is still alive and well in Germany. When the Singapore police located and interviewed him, he was unable to say how his card came to be in Martin's possession; all he knew was that he had lost it and reported it missing. His report prevented the use of the card and this could be the reason why Martin killed tourists for their credit cards. If the owners were dead, they would not be able to report their cards missing, and he would be able to use the cards to withdraw money.

The other man is an unidentified Caucasian traveller whom Martin approached at Changi International Airport on the morning of March 8, 1995, before the unfortunate Lowe came along. This man had declined Martin's offer to travel together. It was only later, when he read about Martin's crimes in the newspapers, that he found out how close he had been to death. He called the Singapore police to relate his experience.

The police wanted him to testify in the High Court. The man, who did not give his name or telephone number, was willing at first but backed out later and did not call again. The experience of this tourist might be a good lesson to others, that one should be wary of unusually nice strangers, especially when travelling in a foreign land.